The Schooner 'Pearl' Incident, 1848

The Schooner 'Pearl' Incident, 1848

Three Accounts of the Largest Recorded Escape Attempt by Slaves in the United States of America

Personal Memoir of Daniel Drayton

Daniel Drayton

(Extract from) The Key to Uncle Tom's Cabin

Harriet Beecher Stowe

The Fugitives of the Pearl

(Extract from "The Journal of Negro History" Vol.1)

John H. Paynter

LEONAUR

The Schooner 'Pearl' Incident, 1848
Three Accounts of the Largest Recorded Escape Attempt by Slaves
in the United States of America
Personal Memoir of Daniel Drayton by Daniel Drayton
(Extract from) The Key to Uncle Tom's Cabin by Harriet Beecher Stowe
and *The Fugitives of the Pearl* by John H. Paynter

FIRST EDITION

First published under the titles
Personal Memoir of Daniel Drayton, for Four Years and Four Months a Prisoner (for Charity's Sake) in Washington Jail Including a Narrative of the Voyage and Capture of the Schooner "Pearl".
(Extract from) The Key to Uncle Tom's Cabin
and
The Fugitives of the Pearl (Extract from The Journal of Negro History Volume 1)

Leonaur is an imprint
of Oakpast Ltd

ISBN: 978-1-78282-134-2 (hardcover)
ISBN: 978-1-78282-135-9 (softcover)

http://www.leonaur.com

Publisher's Notes

The views expressed in this book are not necessarily
those of the publisher.

Contents

Personal Memoir of Daniel Drayton

Contents

WE HOLD THESE TRUTHS TO BE SELF-EVIDENT:

THAT ALL MEN ARE CREATED EQUAL;

THAT THEY ARE ENDOWED BY THEIR CREATOR

WITH CERTAIN UNALIENABLE RIGHTS;

THAT AMONG THESE ARE LIFE, *LIBERTY*,

AND THE PURSUIT OF HAPPINESS.

DECLARATION OF INDEPENDENCE.

Advertisement

Considering the large share of the public attention which the case of the schooner *Pearl* attracted at the time of its occurrence, perhaps the following narrative of its origin, and of its consequences to himself, by the principal actor in it, may not be without interest. It is proper to state that a large share of the profits of the sale are secured to Captain Drayton, the state of whose health incapacitates him from any laborious employment.

Memoir

I was born in the year 1802, in Cumberland County, Downs Township, in the State of New Jersey, on the shores of Nantuxet Creek, not far from Delaware Bay, into which that creek flows. My father was a farmer,—not a very profitable occupation in that barren part of the country. My mother was a widow at the time of her marriage with my father, having three children by a former husband. By my father she had six more, of whom I was the youngest but one. She was a woman of strong mind and marked character, a zealous member of the Methodist church; and, although I had the misfortune to lose her at an early age, her instructions—though the effect was not apparent at the moment—made a deep impression on my youthful mind, and no doubt had a very sensible influence over my future life.

Just previous to, or during the war with Great Britain, my father removed still nearer to the shore of the bay, and the sight of the vessels passing up and down inspired me with a desire to follow the life of a waterman; but it was some years before I was able to gratify this wish. I well remember the alarm created in our neighbourhood by the incursions of the British vessels up the bay during the war, and that, at these times, the women of the neighbourhood used to collect at our house, as if looking up to my mother for counsel and guidance.

I was only twelve years old when this good mother died; but, so strong was the impression which she left upon my memory, that, amid the struggles and dangers and cares of my subsequent life, I have seldom closed my eyes to sleep without some thought or image of her.

As my father soon after married another widow, with four small children, it became necessary to make room in the house for their accommodation; and, with a younger brother of mine, I was bound out an apprentice in a cotton and woollen factory at a place called Cedarville. Manufactures were just then beginning to be introduced into the country, and great hopes were entertained of them as a profitable business. My employer,—or boss, as we called him,—had formerly been a schoolmaster, and he did not wholly neglect our instructions in other things be sides cotton-spinning. Of this I stood greatly in need; for there were no public schools in the neighbourhood in which I was born, and my parents had too many children to feed and clothe to be able to pay much for schooling.

We were required on Sundays, by our employer, to learn two lessons, one in the forenoon, the other in the afternoon; after reciting which we were left at liberty to roam at our pleasure. Winter evenings we worked in the factory till nine o'clock, after which, and before going to bed, we were required to recite over one of our lessons.

These advantages of education were not great, but even these I soon lost. Within five months from the time I was bound to him, my employer died. The factories were then sold out to three partners. The one who carried on the cotton-spinning took me; but he soon gave up the business, and went back to farming, which had been his original occupation. I remained with him for a year and a half, or thereabouts, when my father bound me out apprentice to a shoemaker.

My new boss was, in some respects, a remarkable man, but not a very good sort of one for a boy to be bound apprentice to. He paid very little attention to his business, which he seemed to think unworthy of his genius. He was a kind-hearted man, fond of company and frolics, in which he indulged himself freely, and much given to speeches and harangues, in which he had a good deal of fluency. In religion he professed to be a Universalist, holding to doctrines and opinions very different from those which my mother had instilled into me. He ridiculed those opinions, and argued against them, but without converting me to his way of thinking; though, as far as practice went, I was ready enough to imitate his example.

My Sundays were spent principally in taverns, playing at dominos, which then was, and still is, a favourite game in that part of the country; and, as the unsuccessful party was expected to treat, I at times ran up a bill at the bar as high as four or six dollars,—no small indebtedness for a young apprentice with no more means than I had.

As I grew older this method of living grew less and less satisfactory to me; and as I saw that no good of any kind, not even a knowledge of the trade he had undertaken to teach me, was to be got of my present boss, I bought my time of him, and went to work with another man to pay for it. Before I had succeeded in doing that, and while I was not yet nineteen, I took upon myself the still further responsibility of marriage. This was a step into which I was led rather by the impulse of youthful passion than by any thoughtful foresight. Yet it had at least this advantage, that it obliged me to set diligently to work to provide for the increasing family which I soon found growing up around me.

I had never liked the shoemaking business, to which my father had bound me an apprentice. I had always desired to follow the water. The vessels which I had seen sailing up and down the Delaware Bay still haunted my fancy; and I engaged myself as cook on board a sloop, employed in carrying wood from Maurice river to Philadelphia. Promotion in this line is sufficiently rapid; for in four months, after commencing as cook, I rose to be captain. This wood business, in which I remained for two years, is carried on by vessels of from thirty to sixty tons, known as bay-craft. They are built so as to draw but little water, which is their chief distinction from the coasters, which are fit for the open sea.

They will carry from twenty-five to fifty cords of wood, on which a profit is expected of a dollar and upwards. They have usually about three hands, the captain, or skipper, included. The men used to be hired, when I entered the business, for eight or ten dollars the month, but they now get nearly or quite twice as much. The captain usually sails the vessel on shares (unless he is himself owner in whole, or in part), victualling the vessel and hiring the men, and paying over to the owner forty dollars out of every hundred. During the winter, from December to March, the navigation is impeded by ice, and the bay-craft seldom run. The men commonly spend this long vacation in visiting, husking-frolics, rabbiting, and too often in taverns, to the exhaustion of their purses, the impoverishment of their families, and the sacrifice of their sobriety.

Yet the watermen, if many of them are not able always to resist the temptations held out to them, are in general an honest and simple-hearted set, though with little education, and sometimes rather rough in their manners. The extent of my education when I took to the water—and in this respect I was not, perhaps, much inferior to the generality of my brother watermen—was to read with no great fluency, and to sign my name; nor did I ever learn much more than this till my residence in Washington jail, to be related hereafter.

Having followed the wood business for two years, I aspired to something a little higher, and obtained the command of a sloop engaged in the coasting business, from Philadelphia southward and eastward. At this time a sloop of sixty tons was considered a very respectable coaster. The business is now mostly carried on by vessels of a larger class: some of them, especially the regular lines of packets, being very handsome and expensive. The terms on which these coasters were sailed were very similar to those already stated in the case of the bay-craft. The captain victualled the vessel, and paid the hands, and received for his share half the net profits, after deducting the extra expenses of loading and unloading.

It was in this coasting business that the best years of my life were spent, during which time I visited most of the ports and rivers between Savannah southward, and St. John, in the British province of New Brunswick, eastward;—those two places forming the extreme limits of my voyagings. As Philadelphia was the port from and to which I sailed, I presently found it convenient to remove my family thither, and there they continued to live till after my release from the Washington prison.

I was so successful in my new business, that, besides supporting my family, I was able to become half owner of the sloop *Superior*, at an expense of over a thousand dollars, most of which I paid down. But this proved a very unfortunate investment. On her second trip after I had bought into her, returning from Baltimore to Philadelphia by the way of the Delaware and Chesapeake canal, while off the mouth of the Susquehanna, she struck, as I suppose, a sunken tree, brought down by a heavy freshet in that river. The water flowed fast into the cabin. It was in vain that I attempted to run her ashore. She sunk in five minutes. The men saved themselves in the boat, which was on deck, and which floated as she went down. I stood by the rudder till the last, and stepped off it into the boat, loath enough to leave my vessel, on which there was no insurance.

By this unfortunate accident I lost everything except the clothes I had on, and was obliged to commence anew. I accordingly obtained the command of the new sloop *Sarah Henry*, of seventy tons burden, and continued to sail her for several years, on shares. While in her I made a voyage to Savannah; and while under sail from that city for Charleston, I was taken with the yellow fever. I lay for a week quite unconscious of anything that was going on about me and came as near dying as a man could do and escape. The religious instructions of my mother had from time to time recurred to my mind, and had occasioned me some anxiety.

I was now greatly alarmed at the idea of dying in my sins, from

16

which I seemed to have escaped so narrowly. My mind was possessed with this fear; and, to relieve myself from it, I determined, if it were a possible thing, to get religion at any rate. The idea of religion in which I had been educated was that of a sudden, miraculous change, in which a man felt himself relieved from the burden of his sins, united to God, and made a new creature. For this experience I diligently sought, and tried every way to get it. I set up family prayers in my house, went to meetings, and conversed with experienced members of the church; but, for nine months or more, all to no purpose. At length I got into an awful state, beginning to think that I had been so desperate a sinner that there was no forgiveness for me.

While I was in this miserable condition, I heard of a camp-meeting about to be held on Cape May, and I immediately resolved to attend it, and to leave no stone unturned to accomplish the object which I had so much at heart. I went accordingly, and yielded myself entirely up to the dictation of those who had the control of the meeting. I did in everything as I was told; went into the altar, prayed, and let them pray over me. This went on for several days without any result. One evening, as I approached the altar, and was looking into it, I met a captain of my acquaintance, and asked him what he thought of these proceedings; and, as he seemed to approve them, I invited him to go into the altar with me. We both went in accordingly, and knelt down. Pretty soon my friend got up and walked away, saying he had got religion.

I did not find it so easily. I remained at the altar, praying, till after the meeting broke up, and even till one o'clock,—a few acquaintances and others remaining with me, and praying round me, and over me, and for me;—till, at last, thinking that I had done everything I could, I told them pray no more, as evidently there was no forgiveness for me. So I withdrew to a distance, and sat down upon an old tree, lamenting my hard case very seriously. I was sure I had committed the unpardonable sin. A friend, who sat down beside me, and of whom I inquired what he supposed the unpardonable sin was, endeavoured to comfort me by suggesting that, whatever it might be, it would take more sense and learning than ever I had to commit it. But I would not enter into his merriment.

All the next day, which was Sunday, I passed in a most miserable state. I went into the woods alone. I did not think myself worthy or fit to associate with those who had religion, while I was anxious to avoid the company of those who made light of it. Sometimes I would sit down, sometimes I would stand up, sometimes I would walk about. Frequently I prayed, but found no comfort in it.

About sunset I met a friend, who said to me, "Well, our camp-meeting is about ended."

What a misery those few words struck to my heart! "About ended!" I said to myself; "about ended, and I not converted!" A little later, as I was passing along the camp-ground, I saw a woman before me kneeling and praying.

An acquaintance of mine, who was approaching her in an opposite direction, called out to me, "Daniel, help me pray for this woman!" I had made up my mind to make one more effort, and I knelt down and commenced praying; but quite as much for myself as for her. Others gathered about us and joined in, and the interest and excitement became so great, that, after a vain effort to call us off, the regular services of the evening were dispensed with, and the ground was left to us. Things went on in this way till about nine o'clock, when, as suddenly as if I had been struck a heavy blow, I felt a remarkable change come over me.

All my fears and terrors seemed to be instantaneously removed, and my whole soul to be filled with joy and peace. This was the sort of change which I had been taught to look for as the consequence of getting that religion for which I had been struggling so hard. I instantly rose up, and told those about me that I was a converted man; and from that moment I was able to sing and shout and pray with the best of them. In the midst of my exultation who should come up but my old master in the shoemaking trade, of whom I have already given some account. He had heard that I was on the camp-ground in pursuit of religion, and had come to find me out. "Daniel," he said, addressing me by my Christian name, "what are you doing here? Don't make a fool of yourself."

To which I answered, that I had got to be just such a fool as I had long wanted to be; and I took him by the arm, and endeavoured to prevail upon him to kneel down and allow us to pray over him, assuring him that I knew his convictions to be much better than his conduct; that he must get religion, and now was the time. But he drew back, and escaped from me, with promises to do better, which, however, he did not keep.

As for myself, considering, and, as I thought, feeling that I was a converted man, I now enjoyed for some time an extraordinary satisfaction, a sort of offset to the months of agony and misery which I had

18

previously endured. But, though regarding myself as now truly converted, I delayed some time before uniting myself with any particular church. I did not know which to join. This division into so many hostile sects seemed to me unaccountable. I thought that all good Christians should love each other, and be as one family. Yet it seemed necessary to unite myself with some body of Christians; and, as I had been educated a Methodist, I concluded to join them.

I have given the account of my religious experience exactly as it seemed to me at the time, and as I now remember it. It corresponded with the common course of religious experiences in the Methodist church, except that with me the struggle was harder than commonly happens. I did not doubt at the time that it was truly a supernatural change, as much the work of the Spirit as the sudden conversions recorded in the Acts of the Apostles. Others can form their own opinion about it. I will only add that subsequent experience has led me to the belief that the reality of a man's religion is more to be judged of by what he does than by how he feels or what he says.

The change which had taken place in me, however it is to be regarded, was not without a decided influence on my whole future life. I no longer considered myself as living for myself alone. I regarded myself as bound to do unto others as I would that they should do unto me; and it was in attempting to act up to this principle that I became involved in the difficulties to be hereafter related.

Meanwhile I resumed my voyages in the *Sarah Henry*, in which I continued to sail, on shares, for several years, with tolerable success. Afterwards I followed the same business in the schooner *Protection*, in which I suffered another shipwreck. We sailed from Philadelphia to Washington, in the District of Columbia, laden with coal, proceeding down the Delaware, and by the open sea; but, when off the entrance of the Chesapeake, we encountered a heavy gale, which split the sails, swept the decks, and drove us off our course as far south as Ocracoke Inlet, on the coast of North Carolina.

I took a pilot, intending to go in to repair damages; but, owing to the strength of the current, which defeated his calculations, the pilot ran us on the bar. As soon as the schooner's bow touched the ground, she swung round broadside to the sea, which immediately began to break over her in a fearful manner. She filled immediately,—everything on deck was swept away; and, as our only chance of safety, we took to the main-rigging This was about seven o'clock in the evening. Towards morning, by reason of the continual thumping; the mainmast began to work through the vessel, and to settle in the sand, so that it became necessary for us to make our way to the fore-rigging; which we did, not without danger, as one of the men was twice washed off.

About a quarter of a mile inside was a small, low island, on which lay five boats, each manned by five men, who had come down to our assistance; but the surf was so high that they did not venture to approach us; so we remained clinging with difficulty to the rigging till about half-past one, when the schooner went to pieces. The mast to which we were clinging fell, and we were precipitated into the raging surf, which swept us onward towards the island already mentioned. The men there, anticipating what had happened, had prepared for its occurrence; and the best swimmers, with ropes tied round their waists, the other end of which was held by those on shore, plunged in to our assistance.

One of our unfortunate company was drowned, the rest of us came safely to the shore; but we lost everything except the clothes we stood in. The fragments saved from the wreck were sold at auction for two hundred dollars. The people of that neighbourhood treated us with great kindness, and we presently took the packet for Elizabeth City, whence I proceeded to Norfolk, Baltimore, and so home.

I had made up my mind to go to sea no more; but, after remaining on shore for three weeks, and riot finding anything else to do, as it was necessary for me to have the means of supporting my increasing family, I took the command of another vessel, belonging to the same owners, the sloop *Joseph B.* While in this vessel, my voyages were to the east ward. I was engaged in the flour-trade, in conjunction with the owners of the vessel. We bought flour and grain on a sixty days' credit, which I carried to the Kennebec, Portsmouth, Boston, New Bedford, and other eastern ports, calculating upon the returns of the voyage to take up our notes.

I was so successful in this business as finally to become the owner of the *Joseph B.*, which vessel I exchanged away at Portsmouth for the *Sophronia*, a top-sail schooner of one hundred and sixty tons, worth about fourteen hundred dollars. In this vessel 1 made two trips to Boston,—one with coal, and the other with timber. Having unloaded my timber, I took in a hundred tons of plaster, purchased on my own account, intending to dispose of it in the Susquehanna. But on the passage I encountered a heavy storm, which blew the masts out of the vessel, and drove her ashore on the south side of Long Island. We saved our lives; but I lost everything except one hundred and sixty dollars, for which I sold what was left of the vessel and cargo.

Having returned to my family, with but little disposition to try my fortune again in the coasting-trade, one day, being in the horse-market, I purchased a horse and wagon; and, taking in my wife and some of the younger children, I went to pay a visit to the neighbourhood in which I was born. Here I traded for half of a bay-craft, of about sixty tons burden, in which I engaged in the oyster-trade, and other small bay-traffic. Having met at Baltimore the owner of the other half, I bought him out also. The whole craft stood me in about seven hundred dollars. I then purchased three hundred bushels of potatoes, with which I sailed for Fredericksburg, in Virginia; but this proved a losing trip, the potatoes not selling for what they cost me.

At Fredericksburg I took in flour on freight for Norfolk; but my ill-luck still pursued me. In unloading the vessel, the cargo forward being first taken out, she settled by the stern and sprang a leak, damaging fifteen barrels of flour, which were thrown upon my hands. I then sailed for the eastern shore of Virginia, and at a place called Cherrystone traded off my damaged flour for a cargo of pears, with which I sailed for New York. I proceeded safely as far as Barnegat, when I encountered a north-east storm, which drove me back into the Delaware, obliging me to seek refuge in the same Maurice river from which I had commenced my seafaring life in the wood business. But by this time the pears were spoiled, and I was obliged to throw them overboard.

At Cherrystone I had met the owner of a pilot-boat, who had seemed disposed to trade with me for my vessel; and I now returned to that place, and completed the trade; after which I loaded the pilot-boat with oysters and terrapins, and sailed for Philadelphia. This boat was an excellent sailer, but too sharp, and not of burden enough for my business; and I soon exchanged her for half a little sloop, in which I carried a load of water-melons to Baltimore.

By this time I was pretty well sick of the water; and, having hired out the sloop, I set up a shop, at Philadelphia, for the purchase and sale of junk, old iron, &c. &c. But, after continuing in this business for about two years,—my health being bad, and the doctor having advised me to try the water again,—I bought half of another sloop, and engaged in trading up and down Chesapeake Bay. Returning home, towards the close of the season, with the proceeds of the summer's business, I encountered, in the upper part of Chesapeake Bay, a terrible snowstorm, which proved fatal to many vessels then in the bay.

In attempting to make a harbour, the vessel struck the ground, and knocked off her rudder; and, in order to get her off, we were obliged to throw over the deck-load. We drifted about all day, it still blowing and snowing, and at night let go both anchors. So we lay for a night and a day; but, having neither boat, rudder nor provisions, I was finally obliged to slip the anchors and run ashore. I sold my half of her, as she lay, for ninety dollars, which was all that remained to me of my investment and my summer's work.

Not having the means to purchase a boat, my health also continuing quite infirm, the next summer I hired one, and continued the same trade up and down the bay which I had followed the previous summer.

My trading up and down the bay, in the way which I have described, of course brought me a good deal into contact with the slave population. No sooner, indeed, does a vessel, known to be from the north, anchor in any of these waters and the slaves are pretty adroit in ascertaining from what state a vessel comes—than she is boarded, if she remains any length of time, and especially over night, by more or less of them, in hopes of obtaining a passage in her to a land of freedom. During my earlier voyagings, several years before, in Chesapeake Bay, I had turned a deaf ear to all these requests. At that time, according to an idea still common enough, I had regarded the negroes as only fit to be slaves, and had not been inclined to pay much attention to the pitiful tales which they told me of ill-treatment by their masters and mistresses But my views upon this subject had undergone a gradual change.

I knew it was asserted in the Declaration of Independence that all men are born free and equal, and I had read in the Bible that God had made of one flesh all the nations of the earth. I had found out, by intercourse with the negroes, that they had the same desires, wishes and hopes, as myself. I knew very well that I should not like to be a slave even to the best of masters, and still less to such sort of masters as the greater part of the slaves seemed to have. The idea of having first one child and then another taken from me, as fast as they grew large enough, and handed over to the slave-traders, to be carried I knew not where, and sold, if they were girls, I knew not for what purposes, would have been horrible enough; and, from instances which came to my notice, I perceived that it was not less horrible and distressing to the parties concerned in the case of black people than of white ones.

I had never read any abolition books, nor heard any abolition lectures. I had frequented only Methodist meetings, and nothing was heard there about slavery. But, for the life of me, I could not perceive why the golden rule of doing to others as you would wish them to do to you did not apply to this case. Had I been a slave myself,—and it's not a great while since the Algerines used to make slaves of our sailors, white as well as black,—I should have thought it very right and proper in anybody who would have ventured to assist me in escaping out of bondage; and the more dangerous it might have been to render such assistance, the more meritorious I should have thought the act to be. Why had not these black people, so anxious to escape from their masters, as good a right to their liberty as I had to mine?

I know it is sometimes said, by those who defend slavery or apologise for it, that the slaves at the south are very happy and contented, if left to themselves, and that this idea of running away is only put into their heads by mischievous white people from the north. This will do very well for those who know nothing of the matter personally, and who are anxious to listen to any excuse. But there is not a waterman who ever sailed in Chesapeake Bay who will not tell you that, so far from the slaves needing any prompting to run away, the difficulty is, when they ask you to assist them, to make them take no for an answer. I have known instances where men have lain in the woods for a year or two, waiting for an opportunity to escape on board some vessel.

On one of my voyages up the Potomac, an application was made to me on behalf of such a run away; and I was so much moved by his story, that, had it been practicable for me at that time, I should certainly have helped him off. One or two attempts I did make to assist the flight of some of those who sought my assistance; but none with success, till the summer of 1847, which is the period to which I have brought down my narrative.

I was employed during that summer, as I have mentioned already in trading up and down the Chesapeake, in a hired boat, a small black boy being my only assistant. Among other trips, I went to Washington with a cargo of oysters. While I was lying there, at the same wharf, as it happened, from which the *Pearl* afterwards took her departure, a coloured man came on board, and, observing that I seemed to be from the north, he said he supposed we were pretty much all abolitionists there. I don't know where he got this piece of information, but I think it likely from some southern member of Congress. As I did not check him, but rather encouraged him to go on, he finally told me that he wanted to get passage to the north for a woman and five children.

The husband of the woman, and father of the children, was a free coloured man; and the woman, under an agreement with her master, had already more than paid for her liberty; but, when she had asked him for a settlement, he had only answered by threatening to sell her. He begged me to see the woman, which I did; and finally I made an arrangement to take them away. Their bedding, and other things, were sent down on board the vessel in open day, and at night the woman came on board with her five children and a niece. We were ten days in reaching Frenchtown, where the husband was in waiting for them. He took them under his charge, and I saw them no more; but, since my release from imprisonment in Washington, I have heard that the whole family are comfortably established in a free country, and doing well.

Having accomplished this exploit,—and was it not something of an exploit to bestow the invaluable gift of liberty upon seven of one's fellow-creatures—the season being now far advanced, I gave up the boat to the owner, and returned to my family at Philadelphia. In the course of the following month of February, I received a note from a person whom I had never known or heard of before, desiring me to call at a certain place named in it. I did so, when it appeared that I had been heard of through the coloured family which I had brought off from Washington. A letter from that city was read to me, relating the case of a family or two who expected daily and hourly to be sold, and desiring assistance to get them away. It was proposed to me to undertake this enterprise; but I declined it at this time, as I had no vessel, and because the season was too early for navigation through the canal.

I saw the same person again about a fortnight later, and finally arranged to go on to Washington, to see what could be done. There I agreed to return again so soon as I could find a vessel fit for the enterprise. I spoke with several persons of my acquaintance, who had vessels under their control; but they declined, on account of the danger. They did not appear to have any other objection, and seemed to wish me success. Passing along the street, I met Captain Sayres, and knowing that he was sailing a small bay-craft, called the *Pearl*, and learning from him that business was dull with him, I proposed the enterprise to him, offering him one hundred dollars for the charter of his vessel to Washington and back to Frenchtown, where, according to the arrangement with the friends of the passengers, they were to be met and carried to Philadelphia. This was considerably more than the vessel could earn in any ordinary trip of the like duration, and Sayres closed with the offer. He fully understood the nature of the enterprise.

By our bargain, I was to have, as supercargo, the control of the vessel so far as related to her freight, and was to bring away from Washington such passengers as I chose to receive on board but the control of the vessel in other respects remained with him. Captain Sayres engaged in this enterprise merely as a matter of business. I, too, was to be paid for my time and trouble,—an offer which the low state of my pecuniary affairs, and the necessity of supporting my family, did not allow me to decline. But this was not, by any means, my sole or principal motive. I undertook it out of sympathy for the enslaved, and from my desire to do something to further the cause of universal liberty.

Such being the different ground upon which Sayres and myself stood, I did not think it necessary or expedient to communicate to him the names of the persons with whom the expedition had originated; and, at my suggestion, those persons abstained from any direct communication with him, either at Philadelphia or Washington. Sayres had, as cook and sailor, on board the *Pearl*, a young man named Chester English. He was married, and had a child or two, but was himself as inexperienced as a child, having never been more than thirty miles from the place where he was born. I remonstrated with Sayres against taking this young man with us. But English, pleased with the idea of seeing Washington, desired to go; and Sayres, who had engaged him for the season, did not like to part with him. He went with us, but was kept in total ignorance of the real object of the voyage. He had the idea that we were going to Washington for a load of ship-timber.

We proceeded down the Delaware, and by the canal into the Chesapeake, making for the mouth of the Potomac. As we ascended that river we stopped at a place called Machudock, where I purchased, by way of cargo and cover to the voyage, twenty cords of wood; and with that freight on board we proceeded to Washington, where we arrived on the evening of Thursday, the 13th of April, 1848.

As it happened, we found that city in a great state of excitement on the subject of emancipation, liberty and the rights of man. A grand torchlight procession was on foot, in honour of the new French revolution, the expulsion of Louis-Philippe, and the establishment of a republic in France. Bonfires were blazing in the public squares, and a great outdoor meeting was being held in front of the *Union* newspaper office, at which very enthusiastic and exciting speeches were delivered, principally by southern democratic members of Congress, which body was at that time in session. A full account of these proceedings, with reports of the speeches, was given in the *Union* of the next day. According to this report, Mr. Foote, the senator from Mississippi, extolled the French revolution as holding out:

> . . . . .to the whole family of man a bright promise of the universal establishment of civil and religious liberty.

> . . . . that the age of tyrants and of slavery was rapidly drawing to a close, and that the happy period to be signalized by the *universal emancipation* of man from the fetters of civic oppression, and the recognition in all countries of the great principles of popular sovereignty, equality and brother hood, was at this moment visibly commencing.

Mr. Stanton, of Tennessee, and others, spoke in a strain equally fervid and philanthropic. I am obliged to refer to the *Union* newspaper for an account of these speeches, as I did not hear them myself. I came to Washington, not to preach, nor to hear preached, emancipation, equality and brotherhood, but to put them into practice. Sayres and English went up to see the procession and hear the speeches. I had other things to attend to.

The news of my arrival soon spread among those who had been expecting it, though I neither saw nor had any direct communication with any of those who were to be my passengers. I had some difficulty in disposing of my wood, which was not a very first-rate article, but finally sold it, taking in payment the purchaser's note on sixty days, which I changed off for half cash and half provisions. As the trader to whom I passed the note had no hard bread, Sayres and myself went in the steamer to Alexandria to purchase a barrel,—a circumstance of which it was afterwards attempted to take advantage against us.

It was arranged that the passengers should come on board after dark on Saturday evening, and that we should sail about midnight. I had understood that the expedition had principally originated in the desire to help off a certain family, consisting of a woman, nine children and two grand-children, who were believed to be legally entitled to their liberty. Their case had been in litigation for some time; but, although they had a very good case,—the lawyer whom they employed (Mr. Bradley, one of the most distinguished members of the bar of the district) testified, in the course of one of my trials, that he believed them to be legally free,—yet, as their money was nearly exhausted, and as there seemed to be no end to the law's delay and the pertinacity of the woman who claimed them, it was deemed best by their friends

that they should get away if they could, lest she might seize them una-
wares, and sell them to some trader.

In speaking of this case, the person with whom I communicated
at Washington informed me that there were also quite a number of
others who wished to avail themselves of this opportunity of escaping, and that the number of passengers was likely to be larger than had
at first been calculated upon. To which I replied, that I did not stand
about the number; that all who were on board before eleven o'clock I
should take,—the others would have to remain behind.

Saturday evening, at supper, I let English a little into the secret of
what I intended. I told him that the sort of ship-timber we were going
to take would prove very easy to load and unload; that a number of
coloured people wished to take passage with us down the bay, and that,
as Sayres and myself would be away the greater part of the evening,
all he had to do was, as fast as they came on board, to lift up the hatch
and let them pass into the hold, shutting the hatch down upon them.
The vessel, which we had moved down the river since unloading the
wood, lay at a rather lonely place, called White-house Wharf, from a
whitish-coloured building which stood upon it. The high bank of the
river, under which a road passed, afforded a cover to the wharf, and
there were only a few scattered buildings in the vicinity. Towards the
town there stretched a wide extent of open fields.

Anxious, as might naturally be expected, as to the result, I kept in
the vicinity to watch the progress of events. There was another small
vessel that lay across the head of the same wharf, but her crew were
all black; and, going on board her just at dusk, I informed the skipper
of my business, intimating to him, at the same time, that it would be a
dangerous thing for him to betray me. He assured me that I need have
no fears of him—that the other men would soon leave the vessel, not
to return again till Monday, and that, for himself, he should go below
and to sleep, so as neither to hear nor to see anything.

Shortly after dark the expected passengers began to arrive, coming
stealthily across the fields, and gliding silently on board the vessel. I
observed a man near a neighbouring brick-kiln, who seemed to be
watching them. I went towards him, and found him to be black. He
told me that he understood what was going on, but that I need have
no apprehension of him. Two white men, who walked along the road
past the vessel, and who presently returned back the same way, occasioned me some alarm; but they seemed to have no suspicions of what
was on foot, as I saw no more of them. I went on board the vessel

several times in the course of the evening, and learned from English that the hold was fast filling up. I had promised him, in consideration of the unusual nature of the business we were engaged in, ten dollars as a gratuity, in addition to his wages.

Something past ten o'clock, I went on board, and directed English to cast off the fastenings and to get ready to make sail. Pretty soon Sayres came on board. It was a dead calm, and we were obliged to get the boat out to get the vessel's head round. After dropping down a half a mile or so, we encountered the tide making up the river; and, as there was still no wind, we were obliged to anchor. Here we lay in a dead calm till about daylight. The wind then began to breeze up lightly from the north ward, when we got up the anchor and made sail.

As the sun rose, we passed Alexandria. I then went into the hold for the first time, and there found my passengers pretty thickly stowed. I distributed bread among them, and knocked down the bulkhead between the hold and the cabin, in order that they might get into the cabin to cook. They consisted of men and women, in pretty equal proportions, with a number of boys and girls, and two small children. The wind kept increasing and hauling to the west ward. Off Fort Washington we had to make two stretches, but the rest of the way we run before the wind.

Shortly after dinner, we passed the steamer from Baltimore for Washington, bound up. I thought the passengers on board took particular notice of us; but the number of vessels met with in a passage up the Potomac at that season is so few, as to make one, at least for the idle passengers of a steamboat, an object of some curiosity. Just before sunset, we passed a schooner loaded with plaster, bound up. As we approached the mouth of the Potomac, the wind hauled to the north, and blew with such stiffness as would make it impossible for us to go up the bay, according to our original plan.

Under these circumstances, apprehending a pursuit from Washington, I urged Sayres to go to sea, with the intention of reaching the Delaware by the outside passage. But he objected that the vessel was not fit to go outside (which was true enough), and that the bargain was to go to Frenchtown. Having reached Point Lookout, at the mouth of the river, and not being able to persuade Sayres to go to sea, and the wind being dead in our teeth, and too strong to allow any attempt to ascend the bay, we came to anchor in Cornfield harbour, just under Point Lookout, a shelter usually sought by bay-craft encountering contrary winds when in that neighbourhood.

We were all sleepy with being up all the night before, and, soon after dropping anchor, we all turned in. I knew nothing more till, waking suddenly, I heard the noise of a steamer blowing off steam along side of us. I knew at once that we were taken. The black men came to the cabin, and asked if they should fight. I told them no; we had no arms, nor was there the least possibility of a successful resistance. The loud shouts and trampling of many feet overhead proved that our assailants were numerous. One of them lifted the hatch a little, and cried out, "Niggers, by G—d!" an exclamation to which the others responded with three cheers, and by banging the butts of their muskets against the deck.

A lantern was called for, to read the name of the vessel; and it being ascertained to be the *Pearl*, a number of men came to the cabin-door, and called for Captain Drayton. I was in no great hurry to stir; but at length rose from my berth, saying that I considered myself their prisoner, and that I expected to be treated as such. While I was dressing, rather too slowly for the impatience of those outside, a sentinel, who had been stationed at the cabin-door, followed every motion of mine with his gun, which he kept pointed at me, in great apprehension, apparently, lest I should suddenly seize some dangerous weapon and make at him. As I came out of the cabin-door, two of them seized me, took me on board the steamer and tied me; and they did the same with Sayres and English, who were brought on board, one after the other. The black people were left on board the *Pearl*, which the steamer took in tow, and then proceeded up the river.

To explain this sudden change in our situation, it is necessary to go back to Washington. Great was the consternation in several families of that city, on Sunday morning, to find no breakfast, and, what was worse, their servants missing. Nor was this disaster confined to Washington only. Georgetown came in for a considerable share of it, and even Alexandria, on the opposite side of the river, had not entirely escaped. The persons who had taken passage on board the *Pearl* had been held in bondage by no less than forty-one different persons. Great was the wonder at the sudden and simultaneous disappearance of so many "prime hands," roughly estimated, though probably with considerable exaggeration, as worth in the market not less than a hundred thousand dollars,—and all at "one fell swoop" too, as the district attorney afterwards, in arguing the case against me, pathetically expressed it!

There were a great many guesses and conjectures as to where these people had gone; and how they had gone; but it is very doubtful

29

whether the losers would have got upon the right track, had it not been for the treachery of a coloured hackman, who had been employed to carry down to the vessel two passengers who had been in hiding for some weeks previous, and who could not safely walk down, lest they might be met and recognized. Emulating the example of that large, and, in their own opinion at least, highly moral, religious and respectable class of white people, known as "dough-faces," this hackman thought it a fine opportunity to feather his nest by playing cat's-paw to the slave-holders.

Seeing how much the information was in demand, and anticipating, no doubt, a large reward, he turned informer, and described the *Pearl* as the conveyance which the fugitives had taken; and, it being ascertained that the *Pearl* had actually sailed between Saturday night and Sunday morning, preparations were soon made to pursue her. A Mr. Dodge, of Georgetown, a wealthy old gentleman, originally from New England, missed three or four slaves from his family, and a small steamboat, of which he was the proprietor, was readily obtained.

Thirty-five men, including a son or two of old Dodge, and several of those whose slaves were missing, volunteered to man her; and they set out about Sunday noon, armed to the teeth with guns, pistols, bowie-knives, &c., and well provided with brandy and other liquors. They heard of us on the passage down, from the Baltimore steamer and the vessel loaded with plaster. They reached the mouth of the river, and, not having found the *Pearl*, were about to return, as the steamer could not proceed into the bay without forfeiting her insurance. As a last chance, they looked into Cornfield harbour, where they found us, as I have related. This was about two o'clock in the morning. The *Pearl* had come to anchor about nine o'clock the previous evening. It is a hundred and forty miles from Washington to Cornfield harbour.

The steamer, with the *Pearl* in tow, crossed over from Point Lookout to Piney Point, on the south shore of the Potomac, and here the *Pearl* was left at anchor, a part of the steamer's company remaining to guard her, while the steamer, having myself and the other white prisoners on board, proceeded up Coan River for a supply of wood, having obtained which, she again, about noon of Monday, took the *Pearl* in tow and started for Washington.

The bearing, manner and aspect of the thirty-five armed persons by whom we had been thus seized and bound, without the slightest shadow of lawful authority, was sufficient to inspire a good deal of alarm. We had been lying quietly at anchor in a harbour of Maryland;

and, although the owners of the slaves might have had a legal right to pursue and take them back, what warrant or authority had they for seizing us and our vessel? They could have brought none from the District of Columbia, whose officers had no jurisdiction or authority in Cornfield harbour; nor did they pretend to have any from the State of Maryland. Some of them showed a good deal of excitement, and evinced a disposition to proceed to lynch us at once.

A man named Houver, who claimed as his property two of the boys passengers on board the *Pearl*, put me some questions in a very insolent tone; to which I replied, that I considered myself a prisoner, and did not wish to answer any questions; whereupon one of the bystanders, flourishing a dirk in my face, exclaimed, "If I was in his place, I'd put this through you!" At Piney Point, one of the company proposed to hang me up to the yard-arm, and make me confess; but the more influential of those on board were not ready for any such violence, though all were exceedingly anxious to get out of me the history of the expedition, and who my employers were. That I had employers, and persons of note too, was taken for granted on all hands; nor did I think it worth my while to contradict it, though I declined steadily to give any information on that point. Sayres and English very readily told all that they knew. English, especially, was in a great state of alarm, and cried most bitterly.

I pitied him much, besides feeling some compunctions at getting him thus into difficulty; and, upon the representations which I made, that he came to Washington in perfect ignorance of the object of the expedition, he was finally untied. As Sayres was obliged to admit that he came to Washington to take away coloured passengers, he was not regarded with so much favour. But it was evidently me whom they looked upon as the chief culprit, alone possessing a knowledge of the history and origin of the expedition, which they were so anxious to unravel. They accordingly went to work very artfully to worm this secret out of me.

I was placed in charge of one Orme, a police-officer of Georgetown, whose manner towards me was such as to inspire me with a certain confidence in him; who, as it afterwards appeared from his testimony on the trial, carefully took minutes—but, as it proved, very confused and incorrect ones—of all that I said, hoping thus to secure something that might turn out to my disadvantage. Another person, with whom I had a good deal of conversation, and who was afterwards produced as a witness against, me, was William H. Craig, in my opinion a much more conscientious person than Orme, who seemed to think that it was part of his duty, as a police-officer, to testify to something, at all hazards, to help on a conviction. But this is a subject to which I shall have occasion to return presently.

In one particular, at least, the testimony of both these witnesses was correct enough. They both testified to my expressing pretty serious apprehensions of what the result to myself was likely to be. What the particular provisions were, in the District of Columbia, as to helping slaves to escape, I did not know; but I had heard that, in some of the slave-states, they were very severe: in fact, I was assured by Craig that I had committed the highest crime, next to murder, known in their laws. Under these circumstances, I made up my mind that the least penalty I should be apt to escape with was confinement in the penitentiary for life; and it is quite probable that I endeavored to console myself, as these witnesses testified, with the idea that, after all, it might, in a religious point of view, be all for the best, as I should thus be removed from temptation, and have ample time for reflection and repentance.

But my apprehensions were by no means limited to what I might suffer under the forms of law. From the temper exhibited by some of my captors, and from the vindictive fury with which the idea of enabling the enslaved to regain their liberty was, I knew, generally regarded at the south, I apprehended more sudden and summary proceedings; and what happened afterwards at Washington proved that these apprehensions were not wholly unfounded. The idea of being torn in pieces by a furious mob was exceedingly disagreeable. Many men, who might not fear death, might yet not choose to meet it in that shape. I called to mind the apology of the Methodist minister, who, just after a declaration of his that he was not afraid to die, ran away from a furious bull that attacked him,—"that, though not fearing death, he did not like to be torn in pieces by a mad bull."

I related this anecdote to Craig, and, as he testified on the trial, expressed my preference to be taken on the deck of the steamer and shot at once, rather than to be given up to a Washington mob to be baited and murdered. I talked pretty freely with Orme and Craig about myself, the circumstances under which I had undertaken this enterprise, my motives to it, my family, my past misfortunes, and the fate that probably awaited me; but they failed to extract from me, what they seemed chiefly to desire, any information which would implicate others. Orme told me, as he afterwards testified, that what the people in the district wanted was the principals; and that, if I would give information that would lead to them, the owners of the slaves would let me go, or sign a petition for my pardon. Craig also made various inquiries tending to the same point.

Though I was firmly resolved not to yield in this particular, yet I was desirous to do all I could to soften the feeling against me; and it was doubtless this desire which led me to make the statements sworn to by Orme and Craig, that I had no connection with the persons called abolitionists,—which was true enough; that I had formerly refused large offers made me by slaves to carry them away and that, in the present instance, I was employed by others, and was to be paid for my services.

On arriving off Fort Washington, the steamer anchored for the night, as the captors preferred to make their triumphant entry into the city by daylight. Sayres and myself were watched during the night by a regular guard of two men, armed with muskets, who were relieved from time to time. Before getting under weigh again,—which they did about seven o'clock in the morning of Tuesday, Feb. 18,—Sayres and myself were tied together arm-and-arm, and the black people also, two-and-two, with the other arm bound behind their backs.

As we passed Alexandria, we were all ordered on deck, and exhibited to the mob collected on the wharves to get a sight of us, who signified their satisfaction by three cheers. When we landed at the steamboat-wharf in Washington, which is a mile and more from Pennsylvania Avenue, and in a remote part of the city, but few people had yet assembled. We were marched up in a long procession, Sayres and myself being placed at the head of it, guarded by a man on each side; English following next, and then the negroes. As we went along, the mob began to increase; and, as we passed Gannon's slave-pen, that slave-trader, armed with a knife, rushed out, and, with horrid imprecations, made a pass at me, which was very near finding its way through my body.

Instead of being arrested, as he ought to have been, this slave-dealer was politely informed that I was in the hands of the law, to which he replied, "D—n the law!—I have three negroes, and I will give them all for one thrust at this d——d scoundrel!" and he followed along, waiting his opportunity to repeat the blow. The crowd, by this time, was greatly increased. We met an immense mob of several thousand persons coming down Four-and-a-half street, with the avowed intention of carrying us up before the capitol, and making an exhibition of us there. The noise and confusion was very great. It seemed as if the time for the lynching had come.

When almost up to Pennsylvania Avenue, a rush was made upon us,—"Lynch them! lynch them! the d—n villains!" and other such cries, resounded on all sides. Those who had us in charge were greatly alarmed; and, seeing no other way to keep us from the hands of the mob, they procured a hack, and put Sayres and myself into it. The hack drove to the jail, the mob continuing to follow, repeating their shouts and threats. Several thousand people surrounded the jail, filling up the enclosure about it.

Our captors had become satisfied, from the statements made by Sayres and myself, and from his own statements and conduct, that the participation of English in the affair was not of a sort that required any punishment; and when the mob made the rush upon us, the persons having him in charge had let him go, with the intention that he should escape. After a while he had found his way back to the steamboat wharf; but the steamer was gone.

Alone in a strange place, and not knowing what to do, he told his story to somebody whom he met, who put him in a hack and sent him up to the jail. It was a pity he lacked the enterprise to take care of himself when set at liberty, as it cost him four months' imprisonment and his friends some money. I ought to have mentioned before that, on arriving within the waters of the district, Sayres and myself had been examined before a justice of the peace, who was one of the captors; and who had acted as their leader. He had made out a commitment against us, but none against English; so that the persons who had him in charge were right enough in letting him go.

Sayres and myself were at first put into the same cell, but, towards night, we were separated. A person named Goddard, connected with the police, came to examine us. He went to Sayres first. He then came to me, when I told him that, as I supposed he had got the whole story out of Sayres, and as it was not best that two stories should be told, I would say nothing. Goddard then took from me my money. One of the keepers threw me in two thin blankets, and I was left to sleep as I could. The accommodations were not of the most luxurious kind. The cell had a stone floor, which, with the help of a blanket, was to serve also for a bed.

There was neither chair, table, stool, nor any individual piece of furniture of any kind, except a night-bucket and a water-can. I was refused my overcoat and valise, and had nothing but my water-can to make a pillow of. With such a pillow, and the bare stone floor for my bed, looked upon by all whom I saw with apparent abhorrence and terror,—as much so to all appearance, as if I had been a murderer, or taken in some other desperate crime,—remembering the execrations which the mob had belched forth against me, and uncertain whether a person would be found to express the least sympathy for me (which might not, in the existing state of the public feeling, be safe), it may be imagined that my slumbers were not very sound.

Meanwhile the rage of the mob had taken, for the moment, another direction. I had heard it said, while we were coming up in the steamboat, that the abolition press must be stopped; and the mob accordingly, as the night came on, gathered about the office of the *National Era*, with threats to destroy it. Some little mischief was done; but the property-holders in the city, well aware how dependent Washington is upon the liberality of Congress, were unwilling that anything should occur to place the district in bad odour at the north.

Some of them, also, it is but justice to believe, could not entirely give in to the slave-holding doctrine and practice of suppressing free discussion by force; and, by their efforts, seconded by a drenching storm of rain, that came on between nine and ten o'clock, the mob were persuaded to disperse for the present. The jail was guarded that night by a strong body of police, serious apprehensions being entertained, lest the mob, instigated by the violence of many southern members of Congress, should break in and lynch us. Great apprehension, also, seemed to be felt at the jail, lest we might be rescued; and we were subject, during the night, to frequent examinations, to see that all was safe. Great was the terror, as well as the rage, which the abolitionists appeared to inspire.

They seemed to be thought capable, if not very narrowly watched, of taking us off through the roof, or the stone floor, or out of the iron-barred doors; and, from the half-frightened looks which the keepers gave me from time to time, I could plainly enough read their thoughts,—that a fellow who had ventured on such an enterprise as that of the *Pearl* was desperate and daring enough to attempt anything. For a poor prisoner like me, so much in the power of his captors, and without the slightest means, hopes, or even thoughts of escape, it was some little satisfaction to observe the awe and terror which he inspired.

Of the prison fare I shall have more to say, by and by. It is sufficient to state here that it was about on a par with the sleeping accommodations, and hardly of a sort to give a man in my situation the necessary physical vigour. However, I thought little of this at that moment, as I was too sick and excited to feel much disposition to eat.

The Washington prison is a large three-storey stone building, the front part of the lower storey of which is occupied by the guard-room, or jail-office, and by the kitchen and sleeping apartments for the keepers. The back part, shut off from the front by strong grated doors, has a winding stone staircase, ascending in the middle, on each side of which, on each of the three stories, are passageways, also shut off from the staircase, by grated iron doors. The back wall of the jail forms one side of these passages, which are lighted by grated windows. On the other side are the cells, also with grated iron doors, and receiving their light and air entirely from the passages. The passages themselves have no ventilation except through the doors and windows, which answer that purpose very imperfectly. The front second storey, over the guard-room, contains the cells for the female prisoners. The front third storey is the debtors' apartment.

The usage of the jail always has been—except in cases of insubordination or attempted escape, when locking up in the cells by day, as well as by night, has been resorted to as a punishment—to allow the prisoners, during the daytime, the use of the passages, for the benefit of light, air and exercise. Indeed, it is hard to conceive a more cruel punishment than to keep a man locked up all the time in one of these half-lighted, unventilated cells. On the morning of the second day of our confinement, we too were let out into the passage. But we were soon put back again, and not only into separate cells, but into separate passages, so as to be entirely cut off from any communication with each other. It was a long time before we were able to regain the privilege of the passage. But, for the present, I shall pass over the internal economy and administration of the prison, and my treatment in it, intending, further on, to give a general sketch of that subject.

About nine or ten o'clock, Mr. Giddings, the member of Congress from Ohio, came to see us. There was some disposition, I understood, not to allow him to enter the jail; but Mr. Giddings is a man not easily repulsed, and there is nobody of whom the good people at Washington, especially the office holders, who make up so large a part of the population, stand so much in awe as a member of Congress; especially a member of Mr. Giddings' wellknown fearless determination. He was allowed to come in, bringing another person with him, but was followed into the jail by a crowd of ruffians, who compelled the turnkey to admit them into the pas sage, and who vented their rage in execration and threats. Mr. Giddings said that he had understood we were here in jail without counsel or friends, and that he had come to let us know that we should not want for either; and he introduced the person he had brought with him as one who was willing to act temporarily as our counsel.

Not long after, Mr. David A. Hall, a lawyer of the district, came to offer his services to us in the same way. Key, the United States Attorney for the district, and who, as such, had charge of the proceedings against us, was there at the same time. He advised Mr. Hall to leave the jail and go home immediately, as the people outside were furious, and he ran the risk of his life. To which Mr. Hall replied that things had come to a pretty pass, if a man's counsel was not to have the privilege of talking with him. "Poor devils!" said the district attorney, as he went out, "I pity them,—they are to be made scapegoats for others!" Yet the ranker, and virulence, and fierce pertinacity with which this Key afterwards pursued me, did not look much like pity. No doubt he was a good deal irritated at his ill success in getting any information out of me.

The seventy-six passengers found on board the *Pearl* had been committed to the jail as runaways; and Mr. Giddings, on going up to the House, by way of warning, I suppose, to the slave-holders, that they were not to be allowed to have everything their own way, moved an inquiry into the circumstances under which seventy-six persons were held prisoners in the district jail, merely for attempting to vindicate their inalienable rights. Mr. Hale also, in the Senate, in consequence of the threats held out to destroy the *Era* office, and to put a stop to the publication of that paper, moved a resolution of inquiry into the necessity of additional laws for the protection of property in the district.

The fury which these movements excited in the minds of the slave-holders found expression in the editorial columns of the Washington *Union*, in an article which I have inserted below, as forming a curious contrast to the exultations of that print, only a week before, and to which I have had occasion already to refer, over the spread of the principles of liberty and universal emancipation. The violent attack upon Mr. Giddings, because he had visited us three poor prisoners in jail, and offered us the assistance of counsel,—as if the vilest criminals were not entitled to have counsel to defend them,—is well worthy of notice. The following is the article referred to.

37

Those two abolition incendiaries (Giddings and Hale) threw firebrands yesterday into the two houses of Congress. The western abolitionist moved a resolution of inquiry into the transactions now passing in Washington, which brought on a fierce and fiery debate on the part of the southern members, in the course of which Mr. Giddings *was compelled to confess,* on the cross-questioning of Messrs. Venable and Haskell, *that he had visited the three piratical kidnappers now confined in jail, and offered them counsel.* The reply of Mr. Toombs, of Georgia, was scorching to an intense degree.

The abolitionist John P. Hale threw a firebrand resolution into the Senate, calling for additional laws to compel this city to prevent riots. This also gave rise to a long and excited debate.

No question was taken, in either house, before they adjourned. But, in the progress of the discussion in both houses, some doctrines were uttered which are calculated to startle the friends of the Union. Giddings justified the kidnappers, and contended that, though the act was legally forbidden, it was not morally wrong! Mr. Toombs brought home the practical consequences of this doctrine to the member from Ohio in a most impressive manner.

Hale, of the Senate, whilst he was willing to protect the abolitionist, expressed himself willing to relax the laws and weaken the protection which is given to the slave property in this district! Mr. Davis, of Massachusetts, held the strange doctrine, that while he would not disturb the rights of the slave-holders, he would not cease to discuss those rights! As if Congress ought to discuss, or to protect a right to discuss, a domestic institution of the Southern States, with which they had no right to interfere! Why discuss, when they cannot act? Why first lay down an abstract principle, which they intend to violate in practice?

Such fanatics as Giddings and Hale are doing more mischief than they will be able to atone for. Their incessant and impertinent intermeddling with the most delicate question in our social relations is creating the most indignant feelings in the community. The fiery discussions they are exciting are calculated to provoke the very riots which they deprecate. Let these madmen forbear, if they value the tranquillity of our country, and the stability of our Union. We conjure them to forbear their maddened, parricidal hand.

An article like this in the *Union* was well calculated, and probably was intended, to encourage and stimulate the rioters, and accordingly they assembled that same evening in greater force than before, threatening the destruction of the *Era* office. The publication office of the *Era* was not far from the Patent Office; and the dwelling-house of Dr. Bailey, the editor, was at no great distance. The mob, taking upon themselves the character of a meeting of citizens, appointed a committee to wait upon Dr. Bailey, to require him to remove his press out of the District of Columbia. Of course, as I was locked up in the jail, trying to rest my aching head and weary limbs, with a stone floor for a bed and a water-can for my pillow, I can have no personal knowledge of what transpired on this occasion. But a correspondent of the New York *Tribune*, who probably was an eye-witness, gives the following account of the interview between the committee and Dr. Bailey:—

> Clearing his throat, the leader of the committee stretched forth his hand, and thus addressed Dr. Bailey:
>
> *Mr. Radcliff.*—Sir, we have been appointed as a committee to wait upon you, by the meeting of the citizens of Washington which has assembled this evening to take into consideration the circumstances connected with the late outrage upon our property, and to convey to you the result of the deliberations of that meeting. You are aware of the excitement which now prevails. It has assumed a most threatening aspect. This community is satisfied that the existence of your press among us is endangering the public peace, and they are convinced that the public interests demand its removal. We have therefore waited upon you for the purpose of inquiring whether you are prepared to remove your press by ten o'clock tomorrow morning; and we beseech you, as you value the peace of this district, to accede to our request. (*Loud shouting heard at the Patent Office.*)
>
> *Dr. Bailey.*—Gentlemen: I do not believe you are actuated by any unkind feelings towards me personally; but you must be aware that you are demanding of me the surrender of a great constitutional right,—a right which I have used, but not abused,—in the preservation of which you are as deeply interested as I am. How can you ask me to abandon it, and thus become a party to my own degradation?

Mr. Radcliff.—We subscribe to all that you say. But you see the popular excitement. The consequences of your refusal are inevitable. Now, if you can avert these consequences by submitting to what the people request, although unreasonable, is it not your duty, as a good citizen, to submit? It is on account of the community we come here, obeying the popular feeling which you hear expressed in the distance, and which cannot be calmed, and, but for the course we have adopted, would at this moment be manifested in the destruction of your office. But they have consented to wait till they hear our report. We trust, then, that, as a good citizen, you will respond favourably to the wish of the people.

Another of the Committee.—As one of the oldest, citizens, I do assure you that it is in all kindness we make this request. We come here to tell you that we cannot arrest violence in any other way than by your allowing us to say that you yield to the request of the people. In kindness we tell you that if this thing commences here we know not where it may end. I am for mild measures myself. The prisoners were in my hands, but I would not allow my men to inflict any punishment on them.

Dr. Bailey.—Gentlemen, I appreciate your kindness; but I ask, is there a man among you who, standing as I now stand, the representative of a free press, would accede to this demand, and abandon his rights as an American citizen?

One of the Committee.—We know it is a great sacrifice that we ask of you; but we ask it to appease popular excitement.

Dr. Bailey.—Let me say to you that I am a peace-man. I have taken no measures to defend my office, my house or myself. I appeal to the good sense and intelligence of the community, and stand upon my rights as an American citizen, looking to the law alone for protection.

Mr. Radcliff.—We have now discharged our duty. It has come to this, the people say it must be done, unless you agree to go tomorrow. We now ask a categorical answer,—Will you remove your press?

Dr. Bailey.—I answer: I make no resistance, and I cannot assent to your demand. The press is there—it is undefended—you can do as you think proper.

One of the Committee.—All rests with you. We tell you what will follow your refusal, and, if you persist, all the responsibility must fall upon your shoulders. It is in your power to arrest the arm that is raised to give the blow. If you refuse to do so by a single expression, though it might cost you much, on you be all the consequences.

Dr. Bailey.—You demand the sacrifice of a great right. You—

One of the Committee (interrupting him).—I know it is a hardship; but look at the consequences of your refusal. We do not come here to express our individual opinions. I would myself leave the district tomorrow, if in your place. We now ask of you, Shall this be done? We beg you will consider this matter in the light in which we view it.

Dr. Bailey.—I am one man against many. But I cannot sacrifice any right that I possess. Those who have sent you here may do as they think proper.

One of the Committee.—The whole community is against you. They say here is an evil that threatens them, and they ask you to remove that evil. You say "No!" and of course on your head be all the consequences.

Dr. Bailey.—Let me remind you that we have been recently engaged in public rejoicings. For what have we rejoiced? Because the people in another land have arisen, and triumphed over the despot, who had done—what? He did not demolish presses, but he imprisoned editors. In other words, he enslaved the press. Will you then present to America and the world—

One of the Committee (interrupting him).—If we could stop this movement of the people, we would do it. But you make us unable to do so. We cannot tell how far it will go. After your press is pulled down, we do not know where they will go next. It is your duty, in such a case, to sacrifice your constitutional rights.

Dr. Bailey.—I presume, when they shall have accomplished their object—

Mr. Radcliff (interrupting).—We advise you to be out of the way! The people think that your press endangers their property and their lives; and they have appointed us to tell you so, and ask you to remove it tomorrow; If you say that you will do so, they will retire satisfied. If you refuse, they say they will tear it down. Here is Mr. Boyle, a gentleman of property, and one of our oldest residents. You see that we are united. If you hold out and occupy your position, the men, women and children of the district will universally rise up against you.

Dr. Bailey (addressing himself to his father, a venerable man of more than eighty years of age, who approached the doorway and commenced remonstrating with the committee).—You do not understand the matter, father; these gentlemen are a committee appointed by a meeting assembled in front of the Patent Office. You need not address remonstrances to them. Gentlemen, you appreciate my position. I cannot surrender my rights. Were I to die for it, I cannot surrender my rights! Tell those who sent you hither that my press and my house are undefended—they must do as they see proper. I maintain my rights, and make no resistance!

The committee then retired, and Dr. Bailey re-entered his dwelling. Meanwhile, the shouts of the mob, as they received the reports of the committee, were re-echoed along the streets. A fierce yell greeted the reappearance of Radcliff in front of the Patent Office. He announced the result of the interview with the editor of the *Era.* Shouts, imprecations, blasphemy, burst from the crowd. "Down with the *Era!*" "Now for it!" "Gut the office!" were the exclamations heard on all sides, and the mob rushed tumultuously to Seventh-street.

But a body of the city police had been stationed to guard the building, and the mob finally contented themselves with passing a resolution to pull it down the next day at ten o'clock, if the press was not meanwhile removed.

That same afternoon, we three prisoners had been taken before three justices, who held a court within the jail for our examination. Mr. Hall appeared as our counsel. The examination was continued till the next day, when we were, all three of us, recommitted to jail, on a charge of stealing slaves, our bail being fixed at a thousand dollars for each slave, or seventy-six thousand dollars for each of us.

Meanwhile, both houses of Congress became the scenes of very warm debates, growing out of circumstances connected with our case. In the Senate, Mr. Hale, agreeably to the notice he had given, asked leave to introduce a bill for the protection of property in the District of Columbia against the violence of mobs. This bill, as was stated in the debate, was copied, almost word for word, from a law in force in the State of Maryland (and many other states have—and all ought to have—a similar law), making the cities and towns liable for any property which might be destroyed in them by mob violence.

In the House the subject came up on a question of privilege, raised by Mr. Palfrey, of Massachusetts, who offered a resolution for the appointment of a select committee to inquire into the currently-reported facts that a lawless mob had assembled during the two previous nights, setting at defiance the constituted authorities of the United States, and menacing members of Congress and other persons. In both those bodies the debate was very warm, as anyone interested in it will find, by reading it in the columns of the *Congressional Globe*.

It was upon this occasion, during the debate in the Senate, that Mr. Foote, then a senator from Mississippi, and now governor of that state, whose speech on the French revolution has been already quoted, threatened to join in lynching Mr. Hale, if he ever set foot in Mississippi, whither he invited him to come for that purpose. This part of the debate was so peculiar and so characteristic, showing so well the spirit with which the District of Columbia was then blazing against me, that I cannot help giving the following extract from Mr. Foote's speech, as contained in the official report:

All must see that the course of the senator from New Hampshire is calculated to embroil the confederacy to put in peril our free institutions—to jeopardize that Union which our forefathers established, and which every pure patriot throughout the country desires shall be perpetuated. Can any man be a patriot who pursues such a course? Is he an enlightened friend of freedom, or even a judicious friend of those with whom he affects to sympathize, who adopts such a course? Who does not know that such men are, practically, the worst enemies of the slaves? I do not beseech the gentleman to stop; but, if he perseveres, he will awaken indignation everywhere, and it cannot be that enlightened men, who conscientiously belong to the faction at the north of which he is understood to be the head, can sanction or approve everything that he may do, under the influence of excitement, in this body.

I will close by saying that, if he really wishes glory, and to be regarded as the great liberator of the blacks,—if he wishes to be particularly distinguished in this cause of emancipation, as it is called,—let him, instead of remaining here in the Senate of the

United States, or instead of secreting himself in some dark corner of New Hampshire, where he may possibly escape the just indignation of good men throughout this republic,—let him visit the good State of Mississippi, in which I have the honour to reside, and no doubt he will be received with such shouts of joy as have rarely marked the reception of any individual in this day and generation. I invite him there, and will tell him, beforehand, in all honesty, that he could not go ten miles into the interior before he would grace one of the tallest trees in the forest, with a rope around his neck, with the approbation of every virtuous and patriotic citizen; and that, if necessary, I should myself assist in the operation!

Mr. Hale's reply was equally characteristic:

The honourable senator invites me to visit the State of Mississippi, and kindly informs me that he would be one of those who would act the assassin, and put an end to my career. He would aid in bringing me to public execution,—no, death by a mob! Well, in return for his hospitable invitation. I can only express the desire that he would penetrate into some of the dark corners of New Hampshire; and, if he do, I am much mistaken if he would not find that the people in that benighted region would be very happy to listen to his arguments, and engage in an intellectual conflict with him, in which the truth might be elicited. I think, however, that the announcement which the honourable Senator has made on this floor of the fate which awaits so humble an individual as myself in the State of Mississippi must convince every one of the propriety of the high eulogium which he pronounced upon her, the other day, when he spoke of the high position which she occupied among the states of this confederacy.—But enough of this personal matter. (*See note following*).

★★★★★★

Note:—The following paragraph, which has recently been going the rounds of the newspapers, will serve to show the sort of manners which prevail in the state so fitly represented by Mr. Foote, and how these southern ruffians experience in their own families the natural effect of the bloodthirsty sentiments which they so freely avow:

The Death of Mr. Carneal. The Vicksburg *Sentinel*, of the 13th *ult.*, gives the following account of the shooting of Mr. Thomas Carneal, son-in-law of Governor Foote:

We have abstained thus long from giving any notice of the sad affair which resulted in the death of Mr. Thomas Carneal, the son-in-law of the governor of our state, that we might get the particulars. It seems that the steamer *E. C. Watkins*, with Mr. Carneal as a passenger, landed at or near the plantation of Judge James, in Washington County. Mr. Carneal had heard that the judge was an extremely brutal man to his slaves, and was likewise excited with liquor; and, upon the judge inviting him and others to take a drink with him, Carneal replied that he would not drink with a man who abused his negroes; this the judge resented as an insult, and high words ensued.

The company took their drink, however, all but Mr. Carneal, who went out upon the bow of the boat, and took a seat, where he was sought by Judge James, who desired satisfaction for the insult. Carneal refused to make any, and asked the old gentleman if any of his sons would resent the insult if he was to slap him in the mouth; to which the judge replied that he would do it himself, if his sons would not; whereupon Mr. Carneal struck him in the mouth with the back of his hand.

The judge resented it by striking him across the head with a cane, which stunned Mr. Carneal very much, causing the blood to run freely from the wound. As soon as Carneal recovered from the wound, he drew a bowie-knife, and attacked the judge with it, inflicting several wounds upon his person, some of which were thought to be mortal.

Some gentlemen, in endeavouring to separate the combatants, were wounded by Carneal. When Judge James arrived at his house, bleeding, and in a dying state, as was thought, his son seized a double-barrelled gun, loaded it heavily with large shot, galloped to where the boat was, hitched his horse, and deliberately raised his gun to shoot Carneal, who was sitting upon a cotton-bale. Mr. James was warned not to fire, as Carneal was unarmed, and he might kill some innocent person. He took his gun from his shoulder, raised it again, and fired both barrels in succession, killing Carneal instantly.

It is a sad affair, and Carneal leaves, besides numerous friends, a most interesting and accomplished widow, to bewail his tragical end.

★★★★★★

Such was the savage character of the debate, that even Mr. Calhoun, who was not generally discourteous, finding himself rather hard pressed by some of Mr. Hale's arguments, excused himself from an answer, on the ground that Mr. Hale was a maniac! The slave-holders set upon Mr. Hale with all their force; but, though they succeeded in voting down his bill, it was generally agreed, and anybody may see by the report, that he had altogether the best of the argument. Mr. Palfrey's resolution was also lost; but the boldness with which Giddings and others avowed their opinions, and the freedom of speech which they used on the subject of slavery, afforded abundant proof that the gagging system which had prevailed so long in Congress had come at last to an end.

These movements, though the propositions of Messrs. Hale and Palfrey were voted down, were not without their effect. The Common Council of Washington appointed an acting mayor, in place of the regular mayor, who was sick. President Polk sent an intimation to the clerks of the departments, some of whom had been active in the mobs, that they had better mind their own business and stay at home. Something was said about marines from the Navy Yard; and from that time the riotous spirit began to subside.

Meanwhile, the unfortunate people who had attempted to escape in the *Pearl* had to pay the penalty of their love of freedom. A large number of them, as they were taken out of jail by the persons who claimed to be their owners, were handed over to the slave-traders. The following account of the departure of a portion of these victims for the southern market was given in a letter which appeared at the time in several northern newspapers:

Washington, April 22, 1848.

Last evening, as I was passing the railroad depot, I saw a large number of coloured people gathered round one of the cars, and, from manifestations of grief among some of them, I was induced to draw near and ascertain the cause of it. I found in the car towards which they were so eagerly gazing about fifty coloured people, some of whom were nearly as white as myself.

46

A majority of them were of the number who attempted to gain their liberty last week. About half of them were females, a few of whom had but a slight tinge of African blood in their veins, and were finely formed and beautiful. The men were ironed together, and the whole group looked sad and dejected. At each end of the car stood two ruffianly-looking personages, with large canes in their hands, and, if their countenances were an index of their hearts, they were the very impersonation of hardened villainy itself.

In the middle of the car stood the notorious slave-dealer of Baltimore, Slatter, who, I learn, is a member of the Methodist church, 'in good and regular standing.' He had purchased the men and women around him, and was taking his departure for Georgia. While observing this old, gray-headed villain,—this dealer in the bodies and souls of men,—the chaplain of the Senate entered the car,—a Methodist brother,—and took his brother Slatter by the hand, chatted with him for some time, and seemed to view the heart rending scene before him with as little concern as we should look upon cattle. I know not whether he came with a view to sanctify the act, and pronounce a parting blessing; but this I do know, that he justifies slavery, and denounces anti-slavery efforts as bitterly as do the most hardened slave-dealers.

A Presbyterian minister, who owned one of the fugitives, was the first to strike a bargain with Slatter, and make merchandise of God's image; and many of these poor victims, thus manacled and destined for the southern market, are regular members of the African Methodist church of this city. I did not hear whether they were permitted to get letters of dismission from the church, and of 'recommendation to any church where God, in his providence, might cast their lot.' Probably a certificate from Slatter to the effect that they are Christians will answer every purpose. No doubt he will demand a good price for slaves of this character. Perhaps brother Slicer furnished him with testimonials of their religious character, to help their sale in Georgia. I understand that he was accustomed to preach to them here, and especially to urge upon them obedience to their masters.

Some of the coloured people outside, as well as in the car, were weeping most bitterly. I learned that many families were separated. Wives were there to take leave of their husbands, and husbands of their wives, children of their parents, brothers and sisters shaking hands perhaps for the last time, friends parting with friends, and the tenderest ties of humanity sundered at the single bid of the inhuman slave-broker before them. A husband, in the meridian of life, begged to see the partner of his bosom. He protested that she was free—that she had free papers, and was torn from him, and shut up in the jail. He clambered up to one of the windows of the car to see his wife, and, as she was reaching forward her hand to him, the black hearted villain, Slatter, ordered him down. He did not obey.

The husband and wife, with tears streaming down their cheeks, besought him to let them converse for a moment. But no! a monster more hideous, hardened and savage, than the blackest spirit of the pit, knocked him down from the car, and ordered him away. The bystanders could hardly restrain themselves from laying violent hands upon the brutes. This is but a faint description of that scene, which took place within a few rods of the capitol, under *enactments* recognised by Congress. O! what a revolting scene to a feeling heart, and what a retribution awaits the actors! Will not these wailings of anguish reach the ears of the Most High? '*Vengeance is mine; I will repay, saith the Lord.*'

Of those sent off at this time, several, through the generosity of charitable persons at the north, were subsequently redeemed, among whom were the Edmundson girls, of whom an account is given in the *Key to Uncle Tom's Cabin*.

From one of the women, who was not sold, but retained at Washington, I received a mark of kindness and remembrance for which I felt very grateful. She obtained admission to the jail, the Sunday after our committal, to see some of her late fellow-passengers still confined there; and, as she passed the passage in which I was confined, she called to me and handed a Bible through the gratings. I am happy to be able to add that she has since, upon a second trial, succeeded in effecting her escape, and that she is now a free woman.

The great excitement which our attempt at emancipation had produced at Washington, and the rage and fury exhibited against us, had the effect to draw attention to our case, and to secure us sympathy and assistance on the part of persons wholly un known to us. A public meeting was held in Faneuil Hall, in Boston, on the 25th of April, at which a committee was appointed, consisting of Samuel May, Samuel G. Howe, Samuel E. Sewell, Richard Hildreth, Robert Morris, Jr., Francis Jackson, Elizur Wright, Joseph Southwick, Walter Channing, J. W. Browne, Henry I. Bowditch, William F. Channing, Joshua P. Blanchard and Charles List, authorized to employ counsel and to collect money for the purpose of securing to us a fair trial, of which, without some interference from abroad, the existing state of public feeling in the District of Columbia seemed to afford little prospect.

A correspondence was opened by this committee with the Hon. Horace Mann, then a representative in Congress from the State of Massachusetts, with ex-Governor Seward, of New York, with Salmon P. Chase, Esq., of Ohio, and with Gen. Fessenden, of Maine, all of whom volunteered their gratuitous services, should they be needed. A moderate subscription was promptly obtained, the larger part of it, as I am informed, through the liberality of Gerrit Smith, now a representative in Congress from New York, whose large pecuniary contributions to all philanthropic objects, as well as his zealous efforts in the same direction both with the tongue and the pen, have made him so conspicuous. He has, indeed, a unique way of spending his large for tune, without precedent, at least in this country, and not likely to find many imitators.

The committee, being thus put in funds, deputed Mr. Hildreth, one of the members of it, to proceed to Washington to make the necessary arrangements. He arrived there toward the end of the month of May, by which time the public excitement against us, or at least the exterior signs of it, had a good deal subsided. But we were still treated with much rigor, being kept locked up in our cells, denied the use of the passage, and not allowed to see anybody, except when once in a while Mr. Giddings or Mr. Hall found an access to us; but even then we were not allowed to hold any conversation, except in the presence of the jailer.

It may well be imagined that the news of my capture and imprisonment, and of the danger in which I seemed to be, had thrown my family into great distress. I also had suffered exceedingly on their account, several of the children being yet too young to shift for themselves. But I was presently relieved, by the information which I received before long, that during my imprisonment my family would be provided for.

Warm remonstrances had been made to the judge of the criminal court by Mr. Hall against the attempt to exclude us from communication with our friends,—a liberty freely granted to all other prisoners. The judge declined to interfere; but Mr. Mann, having agreed to act as our counsel, was thenceforth freely admitted to interviews with us, without the presence of any keeper. Books and newspapers were furnished me by friends out of doors. I presently obtained a mattress, and the liberty of providing myself with better food than the jail allows. I continued to suffer a good deal of annoyance from the capricious insolence and tyranny of the marshal, Robert Wallace; but I intend to go more at length into the details of my prison experience after having first disposed of the legal proceedings against us.

The feeling against me was no doubt greatly increased by the failure of the efforts repeatedly made to induce me to give up the names of those who had cooperated with me, and to turn states-evidence against them. There was a certain Mr. Taylor, from Boston, I believe, then in Washington, the inventor of a submarine armour for diving purposes. I had formerly been well acquainted with him, and, at a time when no friend of mine was allowed access to me, he made me repeated visits at the jail, at the request, as he said, of the district attorney, to induce me to make a full disclosure, in which case it was intimated I should be let off very easy.

As Mr. Taylor did not prevail with me, one of the jailers afterwards assured me that he was authorized to promise me a thousand dollars in case I would become a witness against those concerned with me. As I turned a deaf ear to all these propositions, the resolution seemed to be taken to make me and Sayres, and even English, suffer in a way to be a warning to all similar offenders.

The laws under which we were to be tried were those of the State of Maryland as they stood previous to the year 1800. These laws had been temporarily continued in force over that part of the district ceded by Maryland (the whole of the present district) at the time that the jurisdiction of the United States commenced; and questions of more general interest, and the embarrassment growing out of the existence of slavery, having defeated all attempts at a revised code, these same old laws of Maryland still remain in force, though modified, in some respects, by acts of Congress. In an act of Maryland, passed in the year 1796, and in force in the district, there was a section which seemed to have been intended for precisely such cases as ours. It provided:

That any person or persons who shall hereafter be convicted of giving a pass to any slave, or person held to service, or shall be found to assist, by advice, donation or loan, or otherwise, the transporting of any slave or any person held to service, from this state, or by any other unlawful means depriving a master or owner of the service of his slave or person held to service, for every such offence the party aggrieved shall recover damages in an action on the case, against such offender or offenders, and such offender or offenders shall also be liable, upon indictment, and conviction upon verdict, confession or otherwise, in this state, in any county court where such offence shall happen, to be fined a sum not exceeding two hundred dollars, at the discretion of the court, one-half to the use of the master or owner of such slave, the other half to the county school, if there be any; if there be no such school, to the use of the county.

Accordingly, the grand jury, under the instructions of the district attorney, found seventy-four indictments against each of us prisoners, based on this act, one for each of the slaves found on board the vessel, two excepted, who were runaways from Virginia, and the names of their masters not known. As it would have been possible to have fined us about fifteen thousand dollars apiece upon these indictments, besides costs, and as, by the laws of the district, there is no method of discharging prisoners from jail who are unable to pay a fine, except by an executive pardon, one would have thought that this might have satisfied. But the idea that we should escape with a fine, though we might be kept in prison for life from inability to pay it, was very unsatisfactory. It was desired to make us out guilty of a penitentiary offence at the least; and for that purpose recourse was had to an old, forgotten act of Maryland, passed in the year 1737, the fourth section of which provided:

That any person or persons who, after the said tenth day of September [1737], shall steal any ship, sloop, or other vessel whatsoever, out of any place within the body of any county within this province, of seventeen feet or upwards by the keel, and shall carry the same ten miles or upwards from the place whence it shall be stolen, *or who shall steal any negro or other slave*, or who shall counsel, hire, aid, abet, or command any person or persons to commit the said offences, or who shall be accessories to the said offences, and shall be thereof legally convicted as aforesaid, or outlawed, or who shall obstinately or of malice stand mute, or peremptorily challenge above twenty, shall suffer death as a felon, or felons, and be excluded the benefit of the clergy.

They would have been delighted, no doubt, to hang us under this act; but that they could not do, as Congress, by an act passed in 1831, having changed the punishment of death, inflicted by the old Maryland statutes (except in certain cases specially provided for), into confinement in the penitentiary for not less than twenty years.

To make sure of us at all events, not less than forty-one separate indictments (that being the number of the pretended owners) were found against each of us for stealing slaves.

Our counsel afterwards made some complaint of this great number of indictments, when two against each of us, including all the separate charges in different counts, would have answered as well. It was even suggested that the fact that a fee of ten dollars was chargeable upon each indictment toward the five-thousand-dollar salary of the district attorney might have something to do with this large number. But the district attorney denied very strenuously being influenced by any such motive, maintaining, in the face of authorities produced against him, that this great number was necessary. He thought it safest, I suppose, instead of a single jury on each charge against each of us, to have the chance of a much greater number, and the advantage, besides, of repeated opportunities of correcting such blunders, mistakes and neglects, as the prisoner's counsel might point out.

On the 6th of July, I was arraigned in the criminal court, Judge Crawford presiding, on one of the larceny indictments, to which I pleaded not guilty; whereupon my counsel, Messrs. Hall and Mann, moved the court for a continuance till the next term, alleging the prevailing public excitement, and the want of time to prepare the defence and to procure additional counsel. But the judge could only be persuaded, and that with difficulty, to delay the trial for eighteen days.

When this unexpected information was communicated to the committee at Boston, a correspondence was opened by telegraph with Messrs. Seward, Chase and Fessenden. But Governor Seward had a legal engagement at Baltimore on the very day appointed for the commencement of the trial, and the other two gentlemen had indispensable engagements in the courts of Ohio and Maine. Under these circumstances, as Mr. Hall was not willing to take the responsibility of acting as counsel in the case, and as it seemed necessary to have someone familiar with the local practice, the Boston committee retained the services of J. M. Carlisle, Esq., of the Washington bar, and Mr. Hildreth again proceeded to Washington to give his assistance. Just as the trial was about to commence, Mr. Carlisle being taken sick, the judge was, with great difficulty, prevailed upon to grant a further delay of three days.

This delay was very warmly opposed, not only by the district attorney, but by the same Mr. Radcliff whom we have seen figuring as chairman of the mob-committee to wait on Dr. Bailey, and who had been retained, at an expense of two hundred dollars, by the friends of English, as counsel for him, they thinking it safest not to have his defence mixed up in any way with that of myself and Sayres. Before the three days were out, Governor Seward, having finished his business in Baltimore, hastened to Washington; but, as the rules of the court did not allow more than two counsel to speak on one side, the other counsel being also fully prepared, it was judged best to proceed as had been arranged.

The trials accordingly commenced on Thursday, the 27th of July, upon an indictment against me for stealing two slaves, the property of one Andrew Houver.

The district attorney, in opening his case, which he did in a very dogmatic, overbearing and violent manner, declared that this was no common affair. The rights of property were violated by every larceny, but this case was peculiar and enormous. Other kinds of property were protected by their want of intelligence; but the intelligence of this kind of property greatly diminished the security of its possession. The jury therefore were to give such a construction to the laws and the facts as to subject violators of it to the most serious consequences.

The facts which seemed to be relied upon by the district attorney as establishing the alleged larceny—were that I had come to Washington, and staid from Monday to Saturday, without any ostensible business, when I had sailed away with seventy-six slaves on board, concealed under the hatches, and the hatches battened down; and that when pursued and overtaken the slaves were found on board with provisions enough for a month.

It is true that Houver swore that the hatches were battened down when the *Pearl* was overtaken by the steamer; but in this he was contradicted by every other government witness. This Houver was, according to some of the other witnesses, in a consider able state of excitement, and at the time of the capture he addressed some violent language to me, as already related. He had sold his two boys, after their recapture, to the slave-traders; but had been obliged to buy them back again, at a loss of one hundred dollars, by the remonstrances of his wife, who did not like to part with them, as they had been raised in the family. Perhaps this circumstance made him the more inveterate against me.

As to the schooner being provisioned for a month, the bill of the provisions on board, purchased in Washington, was produced on the trial, and they were found to amount to three bushels of meal, two hundred and six pounds of pork, and fifteen gallons of molasses, which, with a barrel of bread, purchased in Alexandria, would make rather a short month's supply for seventy-nine persons!

It was also proved, by the government witnesses, that the *Pearl* was a mere bay-craft, not fit to go to sea; which did not agree very well with the idea held out by the District Attorney, that I intended to run these negroes off to the West Indies, and to sell them there. But, to make up for these deficiencies, Williams, who acted as the leader of the steamer expedition, swore that I had said, while on board, that if I had got off with the negroes I should have made an independent fortune; but on the next trial he could not say whether it was I who told him so, or whether somebody else told him that I had said so.

Orme and Craig, with whom I principally conversed, and who went into long details, recollected nothing of the sort; and it is very certain that, as there was no foundation for it, and no motive for such a statement on my part, I never made it. Williams, perhaps, had heard somebody guess that, if I had got off, I had slaves enough to make me independent; and that guess of somebody else he perhaps remembered, or seemed to remember, as something said by me, or reported to have been said by me; and such often, in cases producing great public excitement, is the sort of evidence upon which men's lives or liberty is sworn away.

The idea, however, of an intention to run the negroes off for sale, seemed principally to rest on the testimony of a certain Captain Baker, who had navigated the steamer by which we were captured at the mouth of the Potomac, and who saw, as he was crossing over to Coan River for wood, a long, black, suspicious-looking brig, with her sails loose, lying at anchor under Point Lookout, about three miles from our vessel. This was proved, by other witnesses, to be a very common place of anchorage; in fact, that it was common for vessels waiting for the wind, or otherwise, to anchor anywhere along the shores of the bay. But Captain Baker thought otherwise; and he and the district attorney wished the jury to infer that this brig seen by him under Point Lookout was a piratical craft, lying ready to receive the negroes on board, and to carry them off to Cuba!

Besides Houver, Williams, Orme, Craig and Baker, another witness was called to testify as to the sale of the wood, and my having been in Washington the previous summer. Many questions as to evidence arose, and the examination of these witnesses consumed about two days and a half.

In opening the defence, Mr. Mann commenced with some remarks on the peculiarity of his position, growing out of the unexpected urgency with which the case had been pushed to a trial, and the public excitement which had been produced by it. He also alluded to the hardship of finding against me such a multiplicity of indictments,— for what individual, however innocent, could stand up against such an accumulated series of prosecutions, backed by all the force of the nation? Some observations on the costs thus unnecessarily accumulated, and, in particular, on the district attorney's ten-dollar fees, produced a great excitement, and loud denials on the part of that officer.

Mr. Mann then proceeded to remark that, in all criminal trials which he had ever before attended or heard of, the prosecuting officer had stated and produced to the jury, in his opening, the law alleged to be violated. As the District Attorney had done nothing of that sort, he must endeavour to do it for him. Mr. Mann then proceeded to call the attention of the jury to the two laws already quoted, upon which the two sets of indictments were founded. Of both these acts charged against me—the stealing of Houver's slaves, and the helping them to escape from their master—I could not be guilty. The real question in this case was, Which had I done?

To make the act stealing, there must have been—so Mr. Mann maintained—a taking *lucri causa*, as the lawyers say; that is, a design on my part to appropriate these slaves to my own use, as my own property. If the object was merely to help them to escape to a free state, then the case plainly came under the other statute.

In going on to show how likely it was that the persons on board the *Pearl* might have desired and sought to escape, independently of any solicitations or suggestions on my part, Mr. Mann alluded to the meeting in honour of the French revolution, already mentioned, held the very night of the arrival of the *Pearl* at Washington. As he was proceeding to read certain extracts from the speech of Senator Foote on that occasion, already quoted, and well calculated, as he suggested, to put ideas of freedom and emancipation into the heads of the slaves, he was suddenly interrupted by the judge, when the following curious dialogue occurred:

Judge Crawford.—A certain latitude is to be allowed to counsel in this case; but I cannot permit any harangue against slavery to be delivered here.

Carlisle (rising suddenly and stepping forward).—I am sure your honour must be labouring under some strange misapprehension. Born and bred and expecting to live and die in a slave-holding community, and entertaining no ideas different from those which commonly prevail here, I have watched the course of my associate's argument with the closest attention. The point he is making, I am sure, is most pertinent to the case,—a point it would be cowardice in the prisoner's counsel not to make; and I must beg your honour to deliberate well before you undertake to stop the mouths of counsel, and to take care that you have full constitutional warrant for doing so.

Judge Crawford.—I can't permit an harangue against slavery.

Mr. Mann proceeded to explain the point at which he was aiming. He had read these extracts from Mr. Foote's speech, delivered to a miscellaneous collection of blacks and whites, bond and free, assembled before the *Union* office, as showing to what exciting influences the slaves of the district were exposed, independently of any particular pains taken by anybody to make them discontented; and, with the same object in view, he proposed to read some further extracts from other speeches delivered on the same occasion.

District Attorney.—If this matter is put in as evidence, it must first be proved that such speeches were delivered.

Mann.—If the authenticity of the speeches is denied, I will call the Honorable Mr. Foote to prove it.

District Attorney.—What newspaper is that from which the counsel reads?

Mann (holding it up).—The Washington *Union*, of April 19th.

And, without further objection, he proceeded to read some further extracts.

He concluded by urging upon the jury that this case was to be viewed merely as an attempt of certain slaves to escape from their masters, and on my part an attempt to assist them in so doing; and therefore a case under the statute of 1796, punish able with fine; and not a larceny, as charged against me in this indictment.

Several witnesses were called who had known me in Philadelphia, to testify as to my good character. The district attorney was very anxious to get out of these witnesses whether they had never heard me spoken of as a man likely to run away with slaves? And it did come out from one of them that, from the tenor of my conversation, it used sometimes to be talked over, that one day or other it "would heave up" that I had helped off some negro to a free state. But these conversations, the witness added, were generally in a jesting tone; and another witness stated that the charge of running off slaves was a common joke among the watermen.

According to the practice in the Maryland criminal courts,—and the same practice prevails in the District of Columbia,—the judge does not address the jury at all. After the evidence is all in, the counsel, before arguing the case, may call upon the judge to give to the jury instructions as to the law. These instructions, which are offered in writing, and argued by the counsel, the judge can give or refuse, as he sees fit, or can alter them to suit himself; but any such refusal or alteration furnishes ground for a bill of exceptions, on which the case, if a verdict is given against the prisoner, may be carried by writ of error before the Circuit Court of the district, for their revisal.

My counsel asked of the judge no less than four teen instructions on different points of law, ten of which the judge refused to give, and modified to suit himself. Several of these related to the true definition of theft, or what it was that makes a taking larceny.

It was contended by my counsel, and they asked the judge to instruct the jury, that, to convict me of larceny, it must be proved that the taking the slaves on board the *Pearl* was with the intent to convert them to my own use, and to derive a gain from such conversion; and that, if they believed that the slaves were received on board with the design to help them to escape to a free state, then the offence was not larceny, but a violation of the statute of 1796.

This instruction, variously put, was six times over asked of the judge, and as often refused. He was no less anxious than the district attorney to convict me of larceny, and send me to the penitentiary. But, having a vast deal more sense than the district attorney, he saw that the idea that I had carried off these negroes to sell them again for my own profit was not tenable. It was plain enough that my intention was to help them to escape. The judge therefore, who did not lack ingenuity, went to work to twist the law so as, if possible, to bring my case within it. Even he did not venture to say that merely to assist slaves to escape was stealing. Stealing, he admitted, must be a taking, *lucri causa*, for the sake of gain; but—so he told the jury in one of his instructions:—

> This desire of gain need not be to convert the article taken to his—the taker's—own use, nor to obtain for the thief the value in money of the thing stolen. If the act was prompted by a desire to obtain for himself, or another even, other than the owner, a money gain, or any other inducing advantage, a dishonest gain, then the act was a larceny.

And, in another instruction, he told the jury:

> . . . . . that if they believed, from the evidence, that the prisoner, before receiving the slaves on board, imbued their minds with discontent, persuaded them to go with him, and, by corrupt influences and inducements, caused them to come to his ship, and then took and carried them down the river, then the act was a larceny.

Upon these instructions of the judge, to which bills of exceptions were filed by my counsel, the case, which had been already near a week on trial, was argued to the jury. The District Attorney had the opening and the close, and both my counsel had the privilege of speaking. For the following sketch of the argument, as well as of the legal points already noted, I am indebted to the notes of Mr. Hildreth, taken at the time:

> *District Attorney.*—I shall endeavour to be very brief in the opening, reserving myself till I know the grounds of defence. It is the duty of the jury to give their verdict according to the law and evidence; and, so far as I knew public opinion, there neither exists now, nor has existed at any other time, the slightest desire on the part of a single individual that the prisoner should have otherwise than a fair trial. I think, therefore, the solemn warnings by the prisoner's counsel to the jury were wholly uncalled for.
>
> There was, no doubt, an excitement out of doors,—a natural excitement,—at such an amount of property snatched up at one fell swoop; but was that to justify the suggestion to a jury of twelve honest men that they were not to act the part of a mob?

The learned counsel who opened the case for the prisoner has alluded to the disadvantage of his position from the fact that he was a stranger. I acknowledge that disadvantage, and I have attempted to remedy it, and so has the court, by extending towards him every possible courtesy. The prisoner's counsel seems to think I press this matter too hard. But am I to sit coolly by and see the hard-earned property of the inhabitants of this district carried off, and when the felon is brought into court not do my best to secure his conviction?

(*The district attorney here went into a long and laboured defence of the course he had taken in preferring against the prisoner forty-one indictments for larceny, and seventy-four others, on the same state of facts, for transportation. He denied that the forty-one larcenies of the property of different individuals could be included in one indictment, and declared that if the prisoner's counsel would show the slightest authority for it he would give up the case. After going on in this strain for an hour or more, attacking the opposite counsel and defending himself, in what Carlisle pronounced 'the most extraordinary opening argument he had ever heard in his life,' the district attorney came down at last to the facts of the case.*)

In what position is the prisoner placed by the evidence? How is he introduced to the jury by his Philadelphia friends? These witnesses were examined as to his character, and the substance of their testimony is, that he is a man who would steal a negro if he got a chance. He passed for honest otherwise. But he says himself he would steal a negro to liberate him, and the court says it makes no difference whether he steals to liberate or steals to sell. Being caught in the act, he acknowledges his guilt, and says he was a deserter from his God, a backslider, a church-member one year the next, in the Potomac with a schooner, stealing seventy-four negroes!

Why say he took them for gain, if he did not steal them? Why say he knew he should end his days in a penitentiary? Why say if he got off with the negroes he should have realized an independent fortune? Did he not know they were slaves? He chartered the vessel to carry off negroes; and, if they were free negroes, or he supposed them to be, how was he to realize an independent fortune? He was afraid of the excitement at Washington. Why so, if the negroes were not slaves? There was the fact of their being under the hatches, concealed in the hold of the vessel,—did not that prove he meant to steal them?

Add to that the other fact of his leaving at night. He comes here with a miserable load of wood; gives it away; sells it for a note; did not care about the wood, wanted only to get it out; had a longing for a cargo of negroes. The wood was a blind; besides he lied about it;—would he have ever come back to collect his note? But the prisoner's counsel says the slaves might have heard Mr. Foote's torchlight oration, and so have been persuaded to go. A likely story!

They all started off, I suppose, ran straight down to the vessel and got into the hold! Seventy-four negroes all together! But was not the vessel chartered in Philadelphia to carry off negroes? This shows the excessive weakness of the defence. And how did the slaves behave after they were captured? If they had been running away, would they not have been downcast and disheartened? Would not they have said, Now we are taken? On the other hand, according to the testimony of Major Williams, on their way back they were laughing, shouting and eating molasses in large quantities. Nero fiddled when Rome was burning, but did not eat molasses. What a transition, from liberty to molasses!

Then it is proved that the bulkhead between the cabin and the hold was knocked down, and that the slaves went to Drayton and asked if they should fight. Did not that show his authority over them,—that the slaves were under his control, and that he was the master-spirit? It speaks volumes.

(*Here followed a long eulogy on the gallantry and humanity of the thirty-five captors. One man did threaten a little, but he was drunk.*)

The substance of the law, as laid down by the judge, is this: If Drayton came here to carry off these people, and, by machinations, prevailed on them to go with him, and knew they were slaves, it makes no difference whether he took them to liberate, or took them to sell. If he was to be paid for carrying them away, that was gain enough. Suppose a man were to take it into his head that the northern factories were very bad things for the health of the factory-girls, and were to go with a schooner for the purpose of liberating those poor devils by stealing the spindles, would not he be served as this prisoner is served here? Would they not exhaust the law-books to find the severest punishment?

There may be those carried so far by a miserable mistaken philanthropy as even to steal slaves for the sake of setting them at liberty. But this prisoner says he did it for gain. We might look upon him with some respect if, in a manly style, he insisted on his right to liberate them. But he avowedly steals for gain. He lies about it, besides. Even a jury of abolitionists would have no sympathy for such a man. Try him anyhow, by the word of God—by the rules of common honesty—he would be convicted, anyhow. He is presented to the world at large as a rogue and a common thief and liar. There can be no other conception of him. He did it for dishonest gain.

The prisoner must be convicted: He cannot escape. There can be no manner of doubt as to his guilt. I am at a loss, without appearing absurd in my own eyes, to conceive what kind of a defence can be made.

I have not the least sort of feeling against the wretch himself,—I desire a conviction from principle. I have heard doctrines asserted on this trial that strike directly at the rights and liberty of southern citizens. I have heard counsel seeking to establish principles that strike directly at the security of southern property. I feel no desire that this man, as a man, should be convicted; but I do desire that all persons inclined to infringe on our rights of property should know that there is a law here to punish them, and I am happy that the law has been so clearly laid down by the court. Let it be known from Maine to Texas, to earth's widest limits, that we have officers and juries to execute that law, no matter by whom it may be violated!

Mann—for the prisoner—regretted to occupy any more of the jury's time with this very protracted trial. I mentioned, some days since, that the prisoner was liable, under the indictments against him, to eight hundred years imprisonment,—a term hardly to be served out by Methuselah himself; but, apart from any punishment, if his hundred and twenty-five trials are to proceed at this rate, the chance is he will die without ever reaching their termination. The district attorney has dwelt at great length on what passed the other day, and more than once he has pointedly referred to me, in a tone and manner not to be mistaken.

I have endeavoured to conduct this trial according to the principles of law, and to that standard I mean to come up. My client, though a prisoner at this bar, has rights, legal, social, human; and upon those rights I mean to insist. This is the first time in my life that I ever heard a prisoner on trial, and before conviction, denounced as a liar, a thief, a felon, a wretch, a rogue. It is unjust to apply these terms to any man on trial. The law presumes him to be innocent. The feelings of the prisoner ought not to be thus outraged. He is unfortunate; he may be guilty; that is the very point you are to try.

This prisoner is charged with stealing two slaves, the property of Andrew Houver. Did he, or not? That point you are to try by the law and the evidence. Because you may esteem this a peculiarly valuable kind of property, you are not to measure out in this case a peculiar kind of justice. You have heard the evidence; the law for the purposes of this trial you are to take from the judge. But you are not to be led away with the idea that you must convict this prisoner at any rate.

It is a well-established principle that it is better for an indefinite number of guilty men to escape than for one innocent man to be convicted and punished; and for the best of reasons,—for to have the very machinery established for the protection of right turned into an instrument for the infliction of wrong, strikes a more fatal blow at civil society than any number of unpunished private injuries.

Nor is there any danger that the prisoner will escape due punishment for any crimes he may have committed. Be sides this and forty other larceny indictments hanging over his head, there are seventy-four transportation indictments against him. Now, he cannot be guilty of both; and which of these offences, if either, does the evidence against him prove?

Who is this man? Look at him! You see he has passed the meridian of life. You have heard about him from his neighbours. They pronounce him a fair, upright, moral man. No suspicion hitherto was ever breathed against his honesty. He was a professor of religion, and, so far as we know, had walked in all the ordinances and commands of the law blameless. Now, in all cases of doubt, a fair and exemplary character, especially in an elderly man, is a great capital to begin with. This prisoner may have been mistaken in his views as to matters of human right;

but, as to violating what he believed to be duty, there is not the slightest evidence that such was his character, but abundance to the contrary. He is found under circumstances that make him amenable to the law; let him be tried,—I do not gainsay that; but let him have the common sentiments of humanity extended toward him, even if he be guilty.

The point urged against him with such earnestness—I may say vehemence—is, not that he took the slaves merely, but that he took them with design to steal. His confessions are dwelt upon, stated and overstated, as you will recollect. But consider under what circumstances these alleged confessions were made. There are circumstances which make such statements very fallacious. Consider his excitement—his state of health; for it is in evidence that he had been out of health, suffering with some disorder which required his head to be shaved. Consider the armed men that surrounded him, and the imminent peril in which he believed his life to be. It is great injustice to brand him with the foul epithet of liar for any little discrepancies, if such there were, in statements made under such circum stances.

Other matters have been forced in, of a most extraordinary character, to prejudice his case in your eyes. It has been suggested—the idea has been thrown out, again and again—that, under pretence of helping them to freedom, he meant to sell these negroes. This suggestion, which outruns all reason and discretion, is founded on the simple fact of a brig seen lying at anchor in a place of common anchorage, suggesting no suspicious appearance, but as to which you are asked to infer that these seventy-six slaves were to be transported into her, and carried to Cuba or elsewhere for sale. What a monstrous imagination! What a gross libel on that brig, her officers, her crew, her owners, all of whom are thus charged as kidnappers and pirates; and all this baseless dream got up for the purpose of influencing your minds against the prisoner! It marks, indeed, with many other things, the style in which this prosecution is conducted.

Take the law as laid down by the court, and it is necessary for the government to prove, if this indictment is to be sustained, that the prisoner corrupted the minds of Houver's slaves, and induced and persuaded them to go on board his vessel. They were found on board the prisoner's vessel, no doubt; but as to how they came there we have not a particle of evidence. Here is a gap, a fatal gap, in the government's case. By what second-sight are you to look into this void space and time, and to say that Drayton enticed them to go on board?

(*The counsel here read from 1* Starkie on Evidence, *510, &c., to the effect that the prosecution are bound by the evidence to exclude every hypothesis inconsistent with the prisoner's guilt.*)

Now, is it the only possible means of accounting for the presence of Houver's slaves on board to suppose that this prisoner enticed them? Might not somebody else have done it? Might they not have gone without being enticed at all? We wished to call the slaves themselves as witnesses, but the law shuts up their mouths. Can you, without any evidence, say that Drayton enticed them, and that by no other means could they come onboard?

Presumptive evidence, as laid down in the book—an acknowledged and unquestioned authority—from which I have read, ought to be equally strong with the evidence of one unimpeached witness swearing positively to the fact. Are you as sure that Drayton enticed those slaves as if that fact had been positively sworn to by one witness, testifying that he stood by and saw and heard it? If you are not, then, under the law as laid down by the court, you cannot find him guilty.

Thursday, Aug. 13.

Carlisle, for the prisoner.—The sun under which we draw our breath, the soil we tottle over in childhood, the air we breathe, the objects that earliest attract our attention, the whole system of things with which our youth is surrounded, impress firmly upon us ideas and sentiments which cling to us to our latest breath, and modify all our views. I trust I am man enough always to remember this, when I hear opinions expressed and views maintained by men educated under a system different from that prevailing here, no matter how contrary those views and opinions may be to my own.

It may surprise those of you who know me,—the moral atmosphere in which I have grown up, and the opinions which I entertain,—but never have I felt so deep and hearty an interest in the defence of any case as in this. This prisoner I never saw till I came from a sick bed into this court, when I met him for

64

the first time. I had participated strongly in the feeling which in connection with him had been excited in this community. As you well know, I have and could have no sympathy with the motives by which he may be presumed to have been actuated. Why, then, this sudden feeling in his behalf? Not, I assure you, from mercenary motives. His acquittal or his condemnation will make no difference in the compensation I receive for my services.

The overpowering interest I feel in this case originates in the fact that it places at stake the reputation of this district, and, in some respects, of the country itself, of which this city is the political capital. The counsel for the government has dwelt with emphasis on the great amount and value of property placed at hazard by this prisoner. There is something, however, far more valuable than property—a fair, honourable, impartial administration of justice; and of the chivalrous race of the south it may be expected that they will do justice, though the heavens fall! God forbid that the world should point to this trial as a proof that we are so besotted by passion and interest that we cannot discern the most obvious distinctions and that on a slave question with a jury of slave-holders there is no possible chance of justice!

Many, I assure you, will be ready to fasten this charge upon us. It is my hope, my ardent desire, it is your sworn duty, that no step be taken against this prisoner without full warrant of law and evidence. The duty of defence I discharge with pleasure. I could have desired that this prisoner might have been defended entirely by counsel resident in this district. It would have been my pride to have shown to the world that of our own mere motion we would do justice in any case, no matter how delicate, no matter how sore the point the prisoner had touched.

My learned friend, the district attorney, has alluded to the courtesy which he and the court have extended to my associate in this cause. I hope he does not plume himself upon that. A gentleman of my associate's learning, ability, unexceptionable deportment, and high character among his own people, must and will be treated with courtesy wherever he goes. But, at the same time that he boasts of his courtesy, the district attorney takes occasion to charge my associate with gross ignorance of the law. He says the forty-one charges could not have been included in one indictment, and offers to give up the case if we will produce a single authority to that effect. It were easy to produce the authority (see 1 Chitty, C. L. Indictment), but, unfortunately, the district attorney has made a promise which he can't fulfil. The district attorney is mistaken in this matter; at the same time, let me admit that in the management of this case he has displayed an ability beyond his years.

This is the first prosecution ever brought, so far as we can discover, on this slave-stealing statute, either in this district or in Maryland. This statute, of the existence of which few lawyers were aware,—I am sure I was not,—has been waked up, after a slumber of more than a century, and brought to bear upon my client. It is your duty to go into the examination of this novel case temperately and carefully; to take care that no man and no court, upon review of the case, shall be able to say that your verdict is not warranted by the evidence. If the case is made out against the prisoner, convict him; but if not, as you value the reputation of the district and your own souls, beware how you give a verdict against him!

You are not a lynch-law court. It is no part of your business to inquire whether the prisoner has done wrong, and if so to punish him for it. It is your sole business to inquire if he be guilty of this special charge set forth against him in this indictment, of stealing Andrew Houver's two slaves. The law you are not expected to judge of; to enlighten you on that matter, we have prayed instructions from the court, and those instructions, for the purpose of this trial, are to be taken as the law. The question for you is, Does the evidence in this case bring the prisoner within the law as laid down by the court? To bring him within that law, you are not to go upon imagination, but upon facts proved by witnesses; and, it seems to me, you have a very plain duty before you. This is not a thing done in a corner. Take care that you render such a verdict that you will not be ashamed to have it set forth in letters of light, visible to all the world.

There are two offences established by the statutes of Maryland, between which, in this case, it becomes your duty to distinguish. Everything depends on these statutes, because without these statutes neither act is a crime. At common law, there are no such offences as stealing slaves, or transporting slaves. Now, which of these two acts is proved against this prisoner? In some respects they are alike. The carrying the slaves away, the depriving the master of their services, is common to both. But, to constitute the stealing of slaves, according to the law as laid down by the court, there must be something more yet.

There must be a corruption of the minds of the slaves, and a seducing them to leave their masters' service. And does not this open a plain path for this prisoner out of the danger of this prosecution? Where is the least evidence that the prisoner seduced these slaves, and induced them to leave their masters? Has the district attorney, with all his zeal, pointed out a single particle of evidence of that sort? Has he done anything to take this case out of the transportation statute, and to convert it into a case of stealing? He has, to be sure, indulged in some very harsh epithets applied to this prisoner,—epithets very similar to those which Lord Coke indulged in on the trial of Sir Walter Raleigh, and which drew out on the part of that prisoner a memorable retort.

My client is not a Raleigh; but neither, I must be permitted to say, is the district attorney a Lord Coke. I should be sorry to have it go abroad that we cannot try a man for an offence of this sort without calling him a liar, a rogue, a wretch.

(*The district attorney here interrupted, with a good deal of warmth. He insisted that he did not address the prisoner, but the jury, and that it was his right to call the attention of the jury to the evidence proving the prisoner to be a liar, rogue and wretch.*)

Carlisle—I do not dispute the learned gentleman's right. It is a matter of taste; but with you, gentlemen of the jury, these harsh epithets are not to make the difference of a hair. You are to look at the evidence; and where is the evidence that the prisoner seduced and enticed these slaves?

It may happen to any man to have a runaway slave in his premises, and even in his employment. It happened to me to have in my employ a runaway,—one of the best servants, by the way, I ever had. He told me he was free, and I employed him as such. If I had happened to have taken him to Baltimore, there would have been a complete similitude to the case at bar, and, according to the district attorney's logic, I might have been indicted for stealing. Because I had him with me, I am to be presumed to have enticed him from his master!

As to the particular circumstances under which he came into my employment, I might have been wholly unable to show them. Is it not possible to suppose a great number of circumstances under which these slaves of Houver left their master's service and came on board the *Pearl*, without any agency on the part of this prisoner? Now, the government might positively disprove and exclude forty such suppositions; but, so long as one remained which was not excluded, you cannot find a verdict of conviction. The government is to prove that the prisoner enticed and seduced these negroes, and you have no right to presume he did so unless every other possible explanation of the case is positively excluded by the testimony.

Is it so extravagant a supposition that Mr. Foote's speech, and the other torchlight speeches heretofore alluded to, heard by these slaves, or communicated to them, might have so wrought upon their minds as to induce them to leave their masters? I don't say that they had any right to suppose that these declamations about universal emancipation had any reference to them. I am a southern man, and I hold to the southern doctrine. I admit that there is no inconsistency between perfect civil liberty and holding people of another race in domestic servitude. But then it is natural that these people should overlook this distinction, however obvious and important. Nor do they lack wit to apply these speeches to their own case or interest in such matters. I myself have a slave as quick to see distinctions as I am, and who would have made a better lawyer if he had had the same advantages.

It came out the other day, in a trial in this court, that the coloured people have debating-societies among themselves. It was an assault and battery case; one of the disputants, in the heat of the argument, struck the other; but then they have precedents for that in the House of Representatives. Is it an impossible, or improbable, or a disproved supposition, that a number of slaves, having agreed together to desert their masters, or having concerted such a plan with somebody here, Drayton was employed to come and take them away, and that he received them on board without ever having seen one of them? If his confessions are to be taken at all, they are to be taken together; and do they not tend to prove such a state of facts? Drayton says he was hired to come here,—that he was to be paid for taking them away. Does that look as if he seduced them?

(*The counsel here commented at length on Drayton's statements, for the purpose of showing that they tended to prove nothing more than a transportation for hire; and he threw no little ridicule on the 'phantom ship' which the district attorney had conjured up in his opening of the case, but which, in his late speech, he had wholly overlooked.*)

But, even should you find that Drayton seduced these slaves to leave their masters, to make out a case of larceny you must be satisfied that he took them into his possession. Now, what is possession of a slave? Not merely being in company with him. If I ride in a hack, I am not in possession of the driver. Possession of a slave is dominion and control; and where is the slightest evidence that this prisoner claimed any dominion or control over these slaves? The whole question in this case is, Were these slaves stolen, or were they running away with the prisoner's assistance? The mere fact of their being in the prisoner's company throws no light whatever on this matter.

The great point, however, in this case is this,—By the judge's instructions, enticement must be proved. Shall the record of this trial go forth to the world showing that you have found a fact of which there was no evidence?

I believe in my conscience there is a gap in this evidence not to be filled up except by passion and prejudice. If that is so, I hope there is no one so ungenerous, so little of a true southerner, as to blame me for my zeal in this case, or not to rejoice in a verdict of acquittal. It is bad enough that strangers should have got up a mob in this district in relation to this matter. It would, however, be a million times worse if juries cannot be found here cool and dispassionate enough to render impartial verdicts.

District Attorney.—I hope, gentlemen of the jury, you will rise above all out-of-door influence. Make yourselves abolitionists, if you can; but look at the facts of the case. And, looking at those facts, is it necessary for me to open my lips in reply? In a case like this, sustained by such direct testimony, such overwhelming proof, I defy any man,—however crazy on the subject of slavery, unless he be blinded by some film of interest,—to hesitate a moment as to his conclusions.

(*The district attorney here proceeded at great length, and with a great air of offended dignity, to complain of having been schooled and advised by the prisoner's counsel, and to justify the use of the foul epithets he had bestowed on the prisoner.)*

This is not a place for parlour talk. I had chosen the English words that conveyed my meaning most distinctly. It was all very well for the prisoner's counsel to smooth things over; but was I, instead of calling him a liar, to say, he told a fib? When I call him a thief and a felon, do I go beyond the charge of the grand jury in the indictment? If this is stepping over the limits of propriety, in all similar cases I shall do the same. I do not intend to black-guard the prisoner,—I do not delight in using these epithets. My heart is not locked up; I am no Jack Ketch, prosecuting criminals for ten dollars a head. I sympathize with the wretches brought here; but when I choose to call them by their proper names I am not to be accused of bandying epithets.

(The district attorney then proceeded also at great length, and in a high key, to justify his hundred and twenty-five indictments against the prisoner, and to clear himself from the imputation of mercenary motives, on the ground that the business of the year, independently of these indictments, would furnish the utmost amount to which he was entitled. He next referred to the matter of the brig testified to by Captain Baker, which had been made the occasion of much ridicule by the prisoner's counsel. Part of the evidence which he had relied on in connection with the brig had been ruled out; and the law, as laid down by the court, according to which taking to liberate was the same as taking to steal, had made it unnecessary for him, so he said, to dwell on this part of the case. Yet he now proceeded to argue at great length, from the testimony in the case, that there must have been a connection between the brig and the schooner; that, as the schooner was confessedly unseaworthy, and could not have gone out of the bay, it must have been the intention to put the slaves on board the brig, and to carry them off to Cuba or elsewhere and sell them. The testimony to this effect he pronounced conclusive)

The United States have laid before you the clearest possible case. I have just gone through a pretty long term of this court; I see several familiar faces on the jury, and I rely on your intelligence. In fact, the only point of the defence is, that the United States have offered no proof that Drayton seduced and enticed these slaves to come on board the *Pearl*; and that the prisoner's counsel are pleased to call a gap, a chasm, which they say you can't fill up. It is the same gap which occurs in every larceny case. Where can the government produce positive testimony to the taking? That is done secretly, in the dark, and is to be presumed from circumstances. A man is found going off with a bag of chickens,—your chickens. Are you going to presume that the chickens run into his bag of their own accord, and without his agency?

A man is found riding your horse. Are you to presume that the horse came to him of its own accord? and yet horses love liberty,—they love to kick up their heels and run. Yet this would be just as sensible as to suppose that these slaves came on board Drayton's vessel without his direct agency. He came here from Philadelphia for them; they are found on board his vessel; Drayton says he would steal a negro if he could; is not that enough? Then he was here some months before with an oyster-boat, pretending to sell oysters. He pretended that he came for his health. Likely story, indeed! I should like to see the doctor who would recommend a patient to come here in the fall of the year, when the fever and ague is so thick in the marshes that you can cut it with a knife.

Cruising about, eating and selling oysters, at that time of the year, for his health! Nonsense! He was here, at that very time, hatching and contriving that these very negroes should go on board the *Pearl*. But the prisoner's counsel say he might have been employed by others simply to carry them away! Who could have employed him but abolitionists; and did he not say he had no sympathy with abolitionists. So much for that hypothesis. Then, he in fact pleads guilty,—he says he expects to die in the penitentiary. Don't you think he ought to? If there is any chasm here, the prisoner must shed light upon it. If he had employers, who were they? The prisoner's counsel have said that he is not bound to tell; and that the witnesses, if summoned here, would not be compelled to criminate themselves. But shall this prisoner be allowed to take advantage of his own wrong?

As to the metaphysics of the prisoner's counsel about possession, that is easily disposed of. Were not these slaves found in Drayton's possession, and didn't he admit that he took them?

As to the cautions given you about prejudice and passion, I do not think they are necessary. I have seen no sort of excitement here since the first detection of this affair that would prevent the prisoner having a fair trial. Is there any crowd or excitement here? The community will be satisfied with the verdict. There is no question the party is guilty. I never had anything to do with a case sustained by stronger evidence. I don't ask you to give an illegal or perjured verdict. Take the law and the evidence, and decide upon it.

N. B.—The argument being now concluded, and the jury about to go out, some question arose whether the jury should have the written instructions of the court with them; and some inquiry being made as to the practice, one of the jurors observed that in a case in which he had formerly acted as juror the jury had the instructions with them, and he proceeded to tell a funny story about a bottle of rum, told by one of the jurors on that occasion, which story caused him to remember the fact. It may be observed, by the way, that the proceedings of the United States Criminal Court for the District of Columbia are not distinguished for any remarkable decorum or dignity. The jury, in this case, were in constant intercourse, during any little intervals in the trial, with the spectators outside the bar.

The case was given to the jury about three o'clock, p. m., and the court, after waiting half an hour, adjourned.

When the court met, at ten o'clock the next morning, the jury were still out, having remained together all night without being able to agree. Meanwhile the district attorney proceeded to try me on another indictment, for stealing three slaves the property of one William H. Upperman. As this trial was proceeding, about half-past two the jury in the first case came in, and rendered a verdict of *guilty*. They presented rather a haggard appearance, having been locked up for twenty-four hours, and some of them being perhaps a little troubled in their consciences.

The jury, it was understood, had been divided, from the beginning, four for acquittal and eight for conviction. These four were all Irishmen, and perhaps they did not consider it consistent with their personal safety and business interests to persist in disappointing the slave-holding public of that verdict which the district attorney had so imperiously demanded. The agreement, it was understood, had taken place only a few moments before they came in, and had been reached entirely on the strength of Williams' testimony to my having said, that had I got off I should have made an independent fortune. Now, it was a curious coincidence, that at the very moment that this agreement was thus taking place, Williams, again on the stand as a witness on the second trial, wished to take back what he had then sworn to on the first trial, stating that he could not tell whether he had heard me say this, or whether he had heard of my having said it from somebody else. After the rendition of the verdict of the other jury, the second case was again resumed. The evidence varied in only a few particulars from that which had been given in the first case.

There was, in addition, the testimony of Upperman, the pretended owner of the woman and her daughters, one of fifteen, the other nine years old, whom I was charged in this indictment with stealing. This man swore with no less alacrity, and with no less falsehood, than Houver had done before him. He stated that about half-past ten, of that same night that the *Pearl* left Washington, while he was fastening up his house, he saw a man standing on the sidewalk opposite his door, and observed him for some time. Not long after, having gone to bed, he heard a noise of somebody coming downstairs; and, calling out, he was answered by his slave-woman, who was just then going off, though he had no suspicion of it at the time. That man standing on the sidewalk he pretended to recognize as me. He was perfectly certain of it, beyond all doubt and question.

The object of this testimony was, to lead to a conclusion of enticement or persuasion on my part, and so to bring the case within one of the judge's instructions already stated. On a subsequent trial, Upperman was still more certain, if possible, that I was the man. But he was entirely mistaken in saying so. His house was on Pennsylvania Avenue, more than a mile from where the *Pearl* lay, and I was not within a mile of it that night. I dare say Upperman was sincere enough. He was one of your positive sort of men; but his case, like that of Houver, shows that men in a passion will sometimes fall into blunders. I have reason to believe that after the trials were over Upperman became satisfied of his error.

The first trial had consumed a week; the second one lasted four days. The judge laid down the same law as before, and similar exceptions were taken by my counsel. The jury again remained out all night, being long divided,—nine for conviction to three for acquittal; but on the morning of August 9th they came in with a verdict of *guilty*.

Satisfied for the present with these two verdicts against me, the district attorney now proposed to pass over the rest of my cases, and to proceed to try Sayres. My counsel objected that, having been forced to proceed against my remonstrances, I was here ready for trial, and they insisted that all my cases should be now disposed of. They did not prevail, however; and the district attorney proceeded to try Sayres on an indictment for stealing the same two slaves of Houver.

In addition to the former witnesses against me, English was now put upon the stand, the district attorney having first entered *nolle prosequi* upon the hundred and fifteen indictments against him. But he could state nothing except the circumstances of his connection with the affair, and the coming on board of the passengers on Saturday night, as I have already related them. On the other hand, the "phantom brig" story, of which the district attorney had made so great a handle in the two cases against me, was now ruled out, on the ground that the brig could not be brought into the case till some connection had first been shown between her and the *Pearl*. The trial lasted three days. The district attorney pressed for a conviction with no less violence than he had done in my case, assuring the jury that if they did not convict there was an end of the security of slave property. But Sayres had several advantages over me.

My two juries had been citizens of Washington, several of them belonging to a class of loafers who frequent the courts for the sake of the fees to be got as jurymen. Some complaints having been made of this, the officers had been sent to Georgetown and the country districts, and the present jury was drawn from those quarters. Then, again, I was regarded as the main culprit,—the only one in the secret of the transaction; and, as I was already convicted, the feeling against Sayres was much lessened. In fact, the jury in his case, after an absence of half an hour, returned a verdict of *not guilty*.

The district attorney, greatly surprised and vexed, proceeded to try Sayres on another indictment. This trial lasted three days and a half; but, in spite of the efforts of the district attorney, who was more positive, longer and louder, than ever, the jury, in ten minutes, returned a verdict of *not guilty*.

The trials had now continued through nearly four weeks of very hot weather, and both sides were pretty well worn out. Vexed at the two last verdicts, the district attorney threatened to give up Sayres on a requisition from Virginia, which was said to have been lodged for us, some of the alleged slaves belonging there, and we having been there shortly before.

Finally, it was agreed that verdicts should be taken against Sayres in the seventy-four transportation cases, he to have the advantage of carrying the points of law before the Circuit Court, and the remaining larceny indictments against him to be discontinued.

Thus ended the first legal campaign. English was discharged altogether, without trial. Sayres had got rid of the charge of larceny. I had been found guilty on two indictments for stealing, upon which Judge Crawford sentenced me to twenty years imprisonment in the penitentiary; while Sayres, on seventy-four indictments for assisting the escape of slaves, was sentenced to a fine on each indictment of one hundred and fifty dollars and costs, amounting altogether to seven thousand four hundred dollars. But from these judgments an appeal had been taken to the Circuit Court, and meanwhile Sayres and I remained in prison as before.

The hearing before the Circuit Court came on the 26th of November. That court consisted of Chief- justice Cranch, an able and upright judge, but very old and infirm; and Judges Morrell and Dunlap, the latter of whom claimed to be the owner of two of the negroes found on board the *Pearl*.

My cases were argued for me by Messrs. Hildreth, Carlisle and Mann. The district attorney, who was much better fitted to bawl to a jury than to argue before a court, had retained, at the expense of the United States, the assistance of Mr. Bradley, one of the ablest lawyers of the district. The argument consumed not less than three days. Many points were discussed; but that on which the cases turned was the definition of larceny. It resulted in the allowance of several of my bills of exceptions, the overturn of the law of Judge Crawford on the subject of larceny, and the establishment by the Circuit Court of the doctrine on that subject contended for by my counsel; but from this opinion Judge Dunlap dissented. The case of Sayres, for want of time, was postponed till the next term.

A new trial having been ordered in my two cases, everybody supposed that the charge of larceny would now be abandoned, as the Circuit Court had taken away the only basis on which it could possibly rest. But the zeal of the District Attorney was not yet satisfied; and, no longer trusting to his own unassisted efforts, he obtained (at the expense of the United States) the assistance of Richard Cox, Esq., an old and very unscrupulous practitioner, with whose aid he tried the cases over again in the Criminal Court. The two trials lasted about fourteen days. I was again defended by Messrs. Mann and Carlisle, and now with better success, as the juries, under the instructions which Judge Crawford found himself obliged to give, and notwithstanding

75

the desperate efforts against me, acquitted me in both cases, almost without leaving their seats.

Finally, the district attorney agreed to abandon the remaining larceny cases, if we would consent to verdicts in the transportation cases on the same terms with those in the case of Sayres. This was done; when Judge Crawford had the satisfaction of sentencing me to fines and costs amounting together to ten thousand and sixty dollars, and to remain in prison until that amount was paid.

There was still a further hearing before the Circuit Court on the bills of exceptions to these transportation indictments. My counsel thought they had some good legal objections; but the hearing unfortunately came on when Judge Cranch was absent from the bench, and the other two judges overruled them. By a strange construction of the laws, no criminal case, except by accident, can be carried before the Supreme Court of the United States; otherwise, the cases against us would have been taken there, including the question of the legality of slavery in the District of Columbia.

Thus, after a severe and expensive struggle, I was saved from the penitentiary; but Sayres and myself remained in the Washington jail, loaded with enormous fines, which, from our total inability to pay them, would keep us there for life, unless the President could be induced to pardon us; and it was even questioned, as I shall show presently, whether he had any such power.

The jail of the District of Columbia is under the charge of the marshal of the district. That office, when I was first committed to prison, was filled by a Mr. Hunter; but he was sick at the time, and died soon after, when Robert Wallace was appointed. This Wallace was a Virginian, from the neighbourhood of Alexandria, son of a Doctor Wallace from whom he had inherited a large property, including many slaves. He had removed to Tennessee, and had set up cotton-planting there; but, failing in that business, had returned back with the small remnants of his property, and Polk provided for him by making him marshal. It was not long before I found that he had a great spite against me.

It was in vain that I solicited from him the use of the passage. The light which came into my cell was very faint, and I could only read by sitting on the floor with my back against the grating of the cell door. But, so far from aiding me to read,—and it was the only method I had of passing my time,—Wallace made repeated and vexatious attempts to keep me from receiving newspapers. I should very soon have died on the prison allowance. The marshal is allowed by the United States thirty-three cents per day for feeding the prisoners. For this money they receive two meals; breakfast, consisting of one herring, corn-bread and a dish of molasses and water, very slightly flavoured with coffee; and for dinner, corn-bread again, with half a pound of the meanest sort of salted beef, and a soup made of corn-meal stirred into the pot-liquor. This is the bill of fare day after day, all the year round; and, as at the utmost such food cannot cost more than eight or nine cents a day for each prisoner, and as the average number is fifty, the marshal must make a handsome profit. The diet has been fixed, I suppose, after the model of the slave allowances.

But Congress, after providing the means of feeding the prisoners in a decent manner, ought not to allow them to be starved for the benefit of the marshal. Such was the diet to which I was confined in the first days of my imprisonment. But I soon contrived to make a friend of Jake, the old black cook of the prison, who, I could see as he came in to pour out my coffee, evinced a certain sympathy and respect for me. Through his agency I was able to purchase some more eatable food; and indeed the surgeon of the jail allowed me flour, under the name of medicine, it being impossible, as he said, for me to live on the prison diet. Wallace, soon after he came into office, finding a small sum in my possession, of about forty dollars, took it from me. He ex pressed a fear that I might corrupt old Jake, or somebody else,—especially as he found that I gave Jake my old newspapers,—and so escape from the prison. But he left the money in the hands of the jailer, and allowed me to draw it out, a dollar at a time.

He presently turned out old Jake, and put in a slave-woman of his own as cook; but she was better disposed towards me than her master, and I found no difficulty in purchasing with my own money, and getting her to prepare such food as I wanted. I was able, too, after some six or eight weeks' sleeping on the stone floor of my cell, to obtain some improvement in that particular; and not for myself only, but for all the other prisoners also. The jailer was requested by several persons who came to see us to procure mattresses for us at their expense; and, finally, Wallace, as if out of pure shame, procured a quantity of husk mattresses for the use of the prisoners generally. Still, we had no cots, and were obliged to spread our mattresses on the floor.

The allowance of clothing made to the prisoners who were confined without any means of supporting themselves corresponded pretty well with the jail allowance of provisions. They received shirts, one at a time, made of the very meanest kind of cotton cloth, and of the very smallest dimensions; trousers of about equal quality, and shoes. It was said that the United States paid also for jackets and caps. How that was I do not know; but the prisoners never received any.

The custody of the jail was intrusted to a head jailer, assisted by four guards, or turnkeys, one of whom acted also as book-keeper. Of the personal treatment toward me of those in office, at the time I was first committed, I have no complaint to make. The rigor of my confinement was indeed great; but I am happy to say that it was not aggravated by any disposition on the part of these men to triumph over me, or to trample upon me. As they grew more acquainted with me, they showed their sense that I was not an ordinary criminal, and treated me with many marks of consideration, and even of regard, and in one of them I found a true friend.

Shortly after Wallace came into office, he made several changes. He was full of caprices, and easily took offence from very small causes; and of this the keepers, as well as the prisoners, had abundant experience. The head jailer did his best to please, behaving in the most humble and submissive manner; but all to no purpose. He was discharged, as were also the others, one after another,—Wallace undertaking to act as head jailer himself. Of Wallace's vexatious conduct towards me; of his refusal to allow me to receive newspapers,—prohibiting the under jailer to lend me even the Baltimore *Sun*; of his accusation against me of bribing old Jake, whom he forbade the turnkeys to allow to come near me; of his keeping me shut up in my cell; and generally of a bitter spirit of angry malice against me,—I had abundant reason to complain during the weary fifteen months or more that I remained under his power.

But his subordinates, though obliged to obey his orders and to comply with his humours, were far from being influenced by his feelings. Even his favourite among the turnkeys, a person who pretty faithfully copied his conduct towards the other prisoners, always behaved very kindly towards me, and even used to make a confidant of me, by coming to my cell to talk over his troubles.

But the person whose kind offices and friendly sympathy did far more than those of any other to relieve the tediousness of my confinement, and to keep my heart from sinking, was Mr. Wood. There is no chaplain at the Washington jail, nor has Congress, so far as I am aware, made any provision of any kind for the spiritual wants or the moral and religious instruction of the inmates of it. This great deficiency Mr. Wood, a man of a great heart, though of very limited pecuniary means, being then a clerk in the Telegraph office, had taken it upon himself to supply, so far as he could; and for that purpose he was in the habit of visiting the prison on Sundays, conversing with the prisoners, and furnishing tracts and books to such as were able and disposed to read. He came to my cell, or to the grating of the passage in which I was confined, on the very first Sunday of my imprisonment, and he readily promised, at my request, to furnish me with a Bible; though in that act of kindness he was anticipated by the coloured woman of whom I have already made mention, who appeared at my cell, with a Bible for me, just after Mr. Wood had left it.

The kindness of Mr. Wood's heart, and the sincerity of his sympathy, was so apparent as to secure him the affectionate respect of all the prisoners. To me he proved a very considerate and useful friend. Not only was I greatly indebted to his assistance in making known my necessities and those of my family to those disposed to relieve them, but his cheerful and Christian conversation served to brighten many a dark hour, and to dispel many gloomy feelings. Were all professing Christians like my friend Mr. Wood, we should not hear so many denunciations as we now do of the church, and complaints of her short-comings.

There was another person, also, whose kind attentions to me I ought not to overlook. This was Mrs. Susannah Ford, a very respectable coloured woman, who sold refreshments in the lobby of the court-house, and who, in the progress of the trial, had evinced a good deal of interest in the case. As she often had boarders in the jail, who, like me, could not live on the jail fare, and whom she supplied, she was frequently there, and she seldom came without bringing with her some substantial token of her regard.

Sayres and myself had looked forward to the change of administration, which resulted from the election of General Taylor, with considerable hopes of advantage from it—but, for a considerable time, this advantage was limited to a change in the marshal in whose custody we were. The turning out of Wallace gave great satisfaction to everybody in the jail, or connected with it, except the turnkeys, who held office by his appointment, and who expected that his dismissal would be followed by their own. The very day before the appointment of his successor came out, I had been remonstrating with him against the cruelty of refusing me the use of the passage; and I had even ventured to hint that I hoped he would do nothing which he would be ashamed to see spoken of in the public prints; to which he replied, "G—d d—n the public prints!—in that cell you will stay!"

But in this he proved not much of a prophet. The next day, as soon as the news of his dismissal reached the jail, the turnkeys at once unlocked my cell-door and admitted me into the pas sage, observing that the new marshal, when he came to take possession, should at least find me there.

This new marshal was Mr. Robert Wallach, a native of the district, very similar in name to his predecessor, but very different in nature; and from the time that he entered into office the extreme rigor hitherto exercised to me was a good deal abated. One thing, however, I had to regret in the change, which was the turning out of all the old guards, with whom I was already well acquainted, and the appointment of a new set. One of these thus turned out—the person to whom I have already referred to as the chief favourite of the late marshal—made a desperate effort to retain his office. But, although he solicited and obtained certificates to the effect that he was, and always had been, a good Whig, he had to walk out with the others.

The new jailer appointed by Wallach, and three of the new guards, or turnkeys, were very gentle manly persons, and neither I nor the other prisoners had any reason to complain of the change. Of the fourth turnkey I cannot say as much. He was violent, overbearing and tyrannical, and he was frequently guilty of conduct towards the prisoners which made him very unfit to serve under such a marshal, and ought to have caused his speedy removal. But, unfortunately, the marshal was under some political obligations to him, which made the turning him out not so easy a matter. This person seemed to have inherited all the feelings of hatred and dislike which the late marshal had entertained towards me, and he did his best to annoy me in a variety of ways, though, of course, his power was limited by his subordinate position.

But, although I gained considerably by the new order of things, I soon found that it had also some annoying consequences. Under the old marshal, either to make the imprisonment more disagreeable to me, or from fear lest I should corrupt the other prisoners, I had been kept in a sort of solitary confinement, no other prisoners being placed in the same pas sage. This system was now altered; and, although my privacy was always so far respected that I was allowed a cell by myself, I often found myself with fellow-prisoners in the same passage from whose society it was impossible for me to derive either edification or pleasure. I suffered a good deal from this cause; but at length succeeded in obtaining a remedy, or, at least, a partial one.

I was allowed, during the daytime, the range of the debtors' apartments, a suite of spacious, airy and comfortable rooms, in which there were seldom more than one or two tenants. I pleaded hard to be removed to these apartments altogether,—to be allowed to sleep there, as well as to pass the days there. As it was merely for the non-payment of a sum of money that I was held, I thought I had a right to be treated as a debtor. But those apartments were so insecure, that the keepers did not care to trust me there during the night.

By this change of quarters my condition was a good deal improved. I not only had ample conveniences for reading, but I improved the opportunity to learn to write, having only been able to sign my name when I was committed to the prison.

But a jail, after all, is a jail; and I longed and sighed to obtain my liberty, and to enjoy again the society of my wife and children. Had it been wished to impress my mind in the strongest manner with the horrors of slavery, no better method could have been devised than this imprisonment in the Washington jail. I felt personally what it was to be restrained of my liberty; and, as many of the prisoners were runaway slaves, or slaves committed at the request of their masters, I saw a good deal of what slaves are exposed to. Of this I shall here give but a single instance.

Wallace, the marshal, as I have already mentioned, had two female slaves, the last remnants of the large slave-property which he had inherited from his father. One of these was a young and very comely mulatto girl, whom Wallace had made his house keeper, and whom he sought to make also his concubine. But, as the girl already had a child by a young white man, to whom she was attached, she steadily repelled all his advances. Not succeeding by persuasion, this scion of the aristocracy of the Old Dominion—this Virginian gentleman, and marshal of the United States for the District of Columbia—shut the girl up in the jail of the district, in hopes of thus breaking her to his will; and, as she proved obstinate, he finally sold her.

He then turned his eyes on the other woman,—his property,— Jemima, our cook, already the mother of three children. But she set him at open defiance. As she wished to be sold, he had lost the greatest means of controlling her; and as she openly threatened, before all the keepers, to tear every rag of clothing off his body if he dared lay his hand upon her, he did not venture to brave her fury.

In most of the states, if not in all of them, certainly in all the free states, there is no such thing as keeping a man in prison for life merely for the non payment of a fine which he has no means to pay. The same spirit of humanity which has abolished the imprisonment of poor debtors at the caprice of their creditors has provided means for discharging, after a short imprisonment, persons held in prison for fines which they have no means of paying. Indeed, what can be more unequal or unjust than to hold a poor man a prisoner for life for an offence which a rich man is allowed to expiate by a small part of his superfluous wealth?

But this is one, among many other barbarisms, which the existence of slavery in the District of Columbia, by preventing any systematic revision of the laws, has entailed upon the capital of our model democracy. There was, as I have stated, no means by which Sayres and myself could be discharged from prison except by paying our fines (which was totally out of the question), or by obtaining a presidential pardon, which, for a long time, seemed equally hopeless. There was, indeed, a peculiarity about our case, such as might afford a plausible excuse for not extending to us any relief. Under the law of 1796, the sums imposed upon us as fines were to go one half to the owners of the slaves, and the other half to the district; and it was alleged, that although the President might remit the latter half, he could not the other.

That same Mr. Radcliff whom I have already had occasion to mention volunteered his services—for a consideration—to get over this difficulty. In consequence of a handsome fee which he received, he undertook to obtain the consent of the owners of the slaves to our discharge. But, having pocketed the money, he made, so far as I could find, very little progress in the business, not having secured above five or six signers. In answer to my repeated applications, he at length proposed that my wife and youngest daughter should come on to Washington to do the business which he had undertaken, and for which he had secured a handsome payment in advance.

They came on accordingly, and, by personal application, succeeded in obtaining, in all, the signatures of twenty-one out of forty-one, the whole number. The reception which they met with from different parties was very different, showing that there is among slave-holders as much variety of character as among other people. Some signed with alacrity, saying that, as no slaves had been lost, I had been kept in jail too long already. Others required much urging. Others positively refused. Some even added insults. Young Francis Dodge, of George town, would not sign, though my life had depended upon it. One wanted me hung, and another tarred and feathered. One pious church-member, lying on his death-bed, as he supposed, was persuaded to sign; but he afterwards drew back, and nothing could prevail on him to put his name to the paper. Die or live, he wholly refused.

But the most curious case occurred at Alexandria, to which place my wife went to obtain the signature of a pious old lady, who had been the claimant of a youngster found among the passengers of the *Pearl*, and who had been sold, in consequence, for the southern market. The old lady, it appeared, was still the owner of the boy's mother, who acted as one of her domestics, and, if she was willing, the old lady professed her readiness to sign. The black woman was accordingly called in, and the nature of my wife's application stated to her. But, with much positiveness and indignation, she refused to give her consent, declaring that my wife could as well do without her husband as she could do without her boy.

So imbruted and stupefied by slavery was this old woman, that she seemed to think the selling her boy away from her a perfectly humane, Christian and proper act, while all her indignation was turned against me, who had merely afforded the boy an opportunity of securing his freedom! I dare say they had persuaded the old woman that I had enticed the boy to run away; whereas, as I have already stated, I had never seen him, nor any other of the passengers, till I found them on board.

As only twenty-one signers could be obtained, the matter stood very much as it did before the attempt was made. So long as President Fillmore remained a candidate for re-election there was little ground to expect from him a favourable consideration of my case. I therefore felt sincerely thankful to the Whig convention when they passed by Mr. Fillmore, and gave the nomination to General Scott. Mr. Fillmore being thus placed in a position which enabled him to listen to the dictates of reason, justice and humanity, my hopes, and those of my friends, were greatly raised. Mr. Sumner, the Free Democratic senator from Massachusetts, had visited me in prison shortly after his arrival at Washington, and had evinced from the beginning a sincere and active sympathy for me.

Some complaints were made against him in some anti-slavery papers, because he did not present to the senate some petitions in my behalf, which had been forwarded to his care. But Mr. Sumner was of opinion, and I entirely agreed with him, that if the object was to obtain my discharge from prison, that object was to be accomplished, not by agitating the matter in the senate, but by private appeals to the equity and the conscience of the President; nor did he think, nor I either, that my interests ought to be sacrificed for the opportunity to make an anti-slavery speech. There is reason in everything; and I thought, and he thought too, that I had been made enough of a martyr of already.

The case having been brought to the notice of the President, he, being no longer a candidate for re-election, could not fail to recognize the claim of Sayres and myself to a discharge. We had already been kept in jail upwards of four years, for an offence which the laws had intended to punish by a trifling pecuniary fine. Nor was this all. The earlier part of our confinement had been exceedingly rigorous, and it had only been by the untiring efforts of our friends, and at a great expense to them, that we had been saved from falling victims to the conspiracy, between the district attorney and Judge Crawford, to send us to the penitentiary.

Although my able and indefatigable counsel, Mr. Mann, whose arduous labours and efforts in my behalf I shall never forget, and still less his friendly counsels and kind personal attentions, had received nothing, except, I believe, the partial reimbursement of his travelling expenses, and although there was much other service gratuitously rendered in our cases, yet it had been necessary to pay pretty roundly for the services of Mr. Carlisle; and, altogether, the expenditures which had been incurred to shield us from the effects of the conspiracy above mentioned far exceeded any amount of fine which might have been reasonably imposed under the indictments upon which we had been found guilty. Was not the enormous sum which Judge Crawford sentenced us to pay a gross violation of the provision in the constitution of the United States against excessive fines? Any fine utterly beyond a man's ability to pay, and which operates to keep him a prisoner for life, must be excessive, or else that word has no meaning.

But, though our case was a strong one, there still remained a serious obstacle in the way, in the idea that, because half the fines was to go to the owners of the slaves, the President could not remit that half. Here was a point upon which Mr. Sumner was able to assist us much more effectually than by making speeches in the senate. It was a point, too, involved in a good deal of difficulty; for there were some English cases which denied the power of pardon under such circumstances. Mr. Sumner found, however, by a laborious examination of the American

84

cases, that a different view had been taken in this co
up and submitted to the President an elaborate lega
the right of the executive to pardon us was very cl

This opinion the President referred to the attor
siderable time elapsed before he found leisure to
last it obtained his sanction, also. Information at l
the matter having been pending for two months
President had signed our pardon. It had yet, howe
the office of the Secretary for the Interior, and meanwhile we were
not by any means free from anxiety. The reader will perhaps recollect
that among the other things which the district attorney had held over
our heads had been the threat to surrender us up to the authorities of
Virginia, on a requisition which it was alleged they had made for us.
The story of this requisition had been repeated from time to time, and
a circumstance now occurred which, in seeming to threaten us with
something of the sort, served to revive all our apprehensions.

Mr. Stuart, the Secretary of the Interior, through whose office the
pardon was to pass, sent word to the marshal that such a pardon had
been signed, and, at the same time, requested him, if it came that day
into his hands, not to act upon it till the next. As this Stuart was a
Virginian, our apprehensions were naturally excited of some movement from that quarter. The pardon arrived about five o'clock that
afternoon; and immediately upon receiving it the marshal told us that
he had no longer any hold upon us,—that we were free men, and at
liberty to go where we chose. As we were preparing to leave the jail, I
observed that a gentle man, a friend of the marshal, whom I had often
seen there, and who had always treated me with great courtesy, hardly
returned my good-day, and looked at me as black as a thunder-cloud.

Afterwards, upon inquiring of the jailer what the reason could be,
I learned that this gentleman, who was a good deal of a politician,
was greatly alarmed and disturbed lest the act of the President in having pardoned us should result in the defeat of the Whig party—and,
though willing enough that we should be released, he did not like
to have it done at the expense of his party, and his own hopes of obtaining some good office. The Whigs were defeated, sure enough: but
whether because we were pardoned—though the idea is sufficiently
flattering to my vanity—is more than I shall venture to decide. The
black prisoners in the jail, having nothing to hope or fear from the rise
or fall of parties, yielded freely to their friendly feelings, and greeted
our departure with three cheers.

the jail as privately as possible, and proceeded in a carriage ...ouse of a gentleman of the district, where we were entertained ...pper. Our imprisonment had lasted four years and four months, ...cking seven days. We did not feel safe, however, with that Virginia requisition hanging over our heads, so long as we remained in the district, or anywhere on slave-holding ground; and, by the liberality of our friends, a hack was procured for us, to carry us, that same night, to Baltimore, there, the next morning, to take the cars for Philadelphia. The night proved one of the darkest and stormiest which it had ever been my fate to encounter,—and I have seen some bad weather in my time.

The rain fell in torrents, and the road was only now and then visible by the flashes of the lightning. But our trusty driver persevered, and, in spite of all obstacles, brought us to Baltimore by the early dawn. Sayres proceeded by the direct route to Philadelphia. Having still some apprehensions of pursuit and a requisition, I took the route by Harrisburg. Great was the satisfaction which I felt as the cars crossed the line from Maryland into Pennsylvania. It was like escaping out of Algiers into a free and Christian country.

I shall leave it to the reader to imagine the meeting between myself and my family. They had received notice of my coming, and were all waiting to receive me. If a man wishes to realize the agony which our American slave-trade inflicts in the separation of families, let him personally feel that separation, as I did; let him pass four years in the Washington jail.

When committed to the prison, I was by no means well. I had been a good deal out of health, as appeared from the evidence on the trial, for two or three years before. Close confinement, or, indeed, confinement of any sort, does not agree with persons of my temperament; and I came out of the prison a good deal older, and much more of an invalid, than when I entered it.

The reader, perhaps, will inquire what good was gained by all these sufferings of myself and my family—what satisfaction I can have, as it did not succeed, in looking back to an enterprise attended with so much risk, and which involved me in so long and tedious an imprisonment?

The satisfaction that I have is this: What I did, and what I attempted to do, was my protest,—a protest which resounded from one end of the Union to the other, and which, I hope, by the dissemination of this, my narrative, to renew and repeat it,—it was my protest against the infamous and atrocious doc trine that there can be any such thing as property in man! We can only do according to our power, and the capacity, gifts and talents, that we have. Others, more fortunate than I, may record their protest against this wicked doctrine more safely and comfortably for themselves than I did.

They may embody it in burning words and eloquent speeches; they may write it out in books; they may preach it in sermons. I could not do that. I have as many thoughts as another, but, for want of education, I lack the power to express them in speech or writing. I have not been able to put even this short narrative on paper without obtaining the assistance of a friend. I could not talk, I could not write; but I could act. The humblest, the most uneducated man can do that. I did act; and, by my actions, I protested that I did not believe that there was, or could be, any such thing as a right of property in human beings.

Nobody in this country will admit, for a moment, that there can be any such thing as property in a white man. The institution of slavery could not last for a day, if the slaves were all white. But I do not see that because their complexions are different they are any the less men on that account. The doctrine I hold to, and which I desired to preach in a practical way, is the doctrine of Jefferson and Madison, that there cannot be property in man,—no, not even in black men. And the rage exerted against me on the part of the slave-holders grew entirely out of my preaching that doctrine. Actions, as everybody knows, speak louder than words. By virtue of my actions proclaiming my opinion on that subject, I became at once, powerless as I otherwise was, el-evated, in the minds of the slave-holders, to the same high level with Mr. Giddings and Mr. Hale, who they could not help believing must have been my secret confederates.

If I had believed, as the slave-holders do, that men can be owned; if I had really attempted, as they falsely and meanly charged me with doing, to steal; had I actually sought to appropriate men as property to my own use; had that been all, does anybody imagine that I should ever have been pursued with such persevering enmity and personal virulence? Do they get up a debate in Congress, and a riot in the city of Washington, every time a theft is committed or attempted in the district? It was purely because I was not a thief; because, in helping men, women and children, claimed as chattels, to escape, I bore my testimony against robbing human beings of their liberty; this was the very thing that excited the slave-holders against me, just as a strong anti-slavery speech excites them against Mr. Hale, or Mr. Giddings, or

Mr. Mann, or Mr. Sumner.

Those gentlemen have words at command; they can speak, and can do good service by doing so. As for me, it was impossible that I should ever be able to make myself heard in Congress, or by the nation at large, except in the way of action. The opportunity occurring, I did not hesitate to improve it; nor have I ever yet seen occasion to regret having done so.

(Extract from) The Key to Uncle Tom's
Cabin

Mary and Emily Edmondson

Contents

THE EDMONDSON SISTERS AND FREDERICK DOUGLASS ATTENDING AN ANTI-SLAVERY CONVENTION IN 1850

(Extract from) The Key to Uncle Tom's Cabin

The next history is a long one, and part of it transpired in a most public manner, in the face of our whole community.

The history includes in it the whole account of that memorable capture of the *Pearl,* which produced such a sensation in Washington in the year 1848. The author, however, will preface it with a short history of a slave-woman who had six children embarked in that ill-fated enterprise.

Milly Edmondson is an aged woman, now upwards of seventy. She has received the slave's inheritance of entire ignorance. She cannot read a letter of a book, nor write her own name; but the writer must say that she was never so impressed with any representation of the Christian religion as that which was made to her in the language and appearance of this woman during the few interviews that she had with her. The circumstances of the interviews will be detailed at length in the course of the story.

Milly is above the middle height, of a large, full figure. She dresses with the greatest attention to neatness. A plain Methodist cap shades her face, and the plain white Methodist handkerchief is folded across the bosom. A well-preserved stuff gown, and clean white apron, with a white pocket-handkerchief pinned to her side, completes the inventory of the costume in which the writer usually saw her. She is a *mulatto,* and must once have been a very handsome one. Her eyes and smile are still uncommonly beautiful, but there are deep-wrought lines of patient sorrow and weary endurance on her face, which tell that this lovely and noble-hearted woman has been all her life a slave.

Milly Edmondson was kept by her owners and allowed to live with her husband, with the express understanding and agreement that her service and value was to consist in bringing up her own children to be sold in the slave-market. Her legal owner was a maiden lady of feeble capacity, who was set aside by the decision of court as incompetent to manage her affairs.

The estate—that is to say, Milly Edmondson and her children—was placed in the care of a guardian. It appears that Milly's poor, infirm mistress was fond of her, and that Milly exercised over her much of that ascendancy which a strong mind holds over a weak one. Milly's husband, Paul Edmondson, was a free man. A little of her history, as she related it to the writer, will now be given in her own words:

"Her mistress," she said, "was always kind to her, 'poor thing!' but then she hadn't *speret* ever to speak for herself, and her friends wouldn't let her have her own way. It always laid on my mind," she said, "that I was a slave. When I wan't more than fourteen years old, Missis was doing some work one day that she thought she couldn't trust me with, and she says to me, 'Milly, now you see it's I that am the slave, and not you.' I says to her, 'Ah, Missis, I am a poor slave for all that.' I's sorry afterwards I said it, for I thought it seemed to hurt her feelings.

"Well, after a while, when I got engaged to Paul, I loved Paul very much; but I thought it wan't right to bring children into the world to be slaves, and I told our folks that I was never going to marry, though I did love Paul. But that wan't to be allowed," she said, with a mysterious air.

"What do you mean?" said I.

"Well, they told me I must marry, or I should be turned out of the church—so it was," she added, with a significant nod.

"Well, Paul and me, we was married, and we was happy enough, if it hadn't been for that; but when our first child was born, I says to him, 'There 'tis, now, Paul, our troubles is begun; this child isn't ours. And every child I had, it grew worse and worse. 'Oh, Paul,' says I, 'what a thing it is to have children that isn't ours!' Paul he says to me, 'Milly, my dear, if they be God's children, it an't so much matter whether they be ours or no; they may be heirs of the kingdom, Milly, for all that.' Well, when Paul's mistress died, she set him free, and he got him a little place out about fourteen miles from Washington; and they let me live out there with him, and take home my tasks; for they had that confidence in me that they always know'd that what I said I'd do was as good done as if they'd seen it done. I had mostly sewing; sometimes a shirt to make in a day—it was coarse like, you know—or a pair of sheets, or some such; but, whatever 'twas, I always got it done. Then I had all my housework and babies to take care of; and many's the time, after ten o'clock, I've took my children's clothes and washed 'em all out and ironed 'em late in the night, 'cause I couldn't never bear to see my children dirty—always wanted to see 'em sweet and clean, and I brought 'em up and taught 'em the very best ways I was able. But nobody knows what I suffered. I never see a white man come on to the place that I didn't think, 'There, now, he's coming to look at my children;' and when I saw any white man going by, I've called in my children and hid 'em, for fear he'd see 'em and want to buy 'em. Oh, ma'am, mine's been a long sorrow, a long sorrow! I've borne this heavy cross a great many years!"

"But," said I, "the Lord has been with you."

She answered, with very strong emphasis, "Ma'am, if the Lord hadn't held me up, I shouldn't have been alive this day. Oh, sometimes my heart's been so heavy, it seemed as if I *must* die; and then I've been to the throne of grace, and when I'd poured out all my sorrows there, I came away *light,* and felt that I could live a little longer!"

This language is exactly her own. She had often a forcible and peculiarly beautiful manner of expressing herself, which impressed what she said strongly.

Paul and Milly Edmondson were both devout communicants in the Methodist Episcopal Church at Washington, and the testimony to their blamelessness of life and the consistence of their piety is unanimous from all who know them. In their simple cottage, made respectable by neatness and order, and hallowed by morning and evening prayer, they trained up their children, to the best of their poor ability, in the nurture and admonition of the Lord, to be sold in the slave-market. They thought themselves only too happy, as one after another arrived at the age when they were to be sold, that they were hired to families in their vicinity, and not thrown into the trader's pen to be drafted for the dreaded Southern market!

The mother, feeling with a constant but repressed anguish the weary burden of slavery which lay upon her, was accustomed, as she told the writer, thus to warn her daughters:—

"Now, girls, don't you never come to the sorrows that I have. Don't you never marry till you get your liberty. Don't you marry to be mothers to *children that an't your own.*"

As a result of this education, some of her older daughters, in connexion with the young men to whom they were engaged, raised the sum necessary to pay for their freedom before they were married.

One of these young women, at the time that she paid for her freedom, was in such feeble health that the physician told her that she could not live many months, and advised her to keep the money, and apply it to making herself as comfortable as she could.

She answered, "If I had only two hours to live, I would pay down that money to die free."

If this was setting an extravagant value on liberty, it is not for an American to say so.

All the sons and daughters of this family were distinguished both for their physical and mental developments, and therefore were priced exceedingly high in the market. The whole family, rated by the market prices which have been paid for certain members of it, might be estimated as an estate of 15,000 dollars. They were distinguished for intelligence, honesty, and faithfulness, but, above all, for the most devoted attachment to each other. These children, thus intelligent, were all held as slaves in the city of Washington, the very capital where our national government is conducted. Of course, the high estimate which their own mother taught them to place upon liberty was in the way of being constantly strengthened and reinforced by such addresses, celebrations, and speeches, on the subject of liberty, as everyone knows are constantly being made, on one occasion or another, in our national capital.

On the 13th day of April, the little schooner *Pearl*, commanded by Daniel Drayton, came to anchor in the Potomac River, at Washington.

The news had just arrived of a revolution in France, and the establishment of a democratic government, and all Washington was turning out to celebrate the triumph of Liberty.

The trees in the avenue were fancifully hung with many-coloured lanterns—drums beat, bands of music played, the houses of the President and other high officials were illuminated, and men, women, and children were all turned out to see the procession, and to join in the shouts of liberty that rent the air. Of course, all the slaves of the city, lively, fanciful, and sympathetic, most excitable as they are by music and by dazzling spectacles, were everywhere listening, seeing, and rejoicing, in ignorant joy. All the heads of departments, senators, representatives, and dignitaries of all kinds, marched in procession to an open space on Pennsylvania Avenue, and there delivered congratulatory addresses on the progress of universal freedom. With unheard-of imprudence, the most earnest defenders of slave-holding institutions poured down on the listening crowd both of black and white, bond and free, the most inflammatory and incendiary sentiments. Such, for example, as the following language of Hon. Frederick P. Stanton, of Tennessee:—

> We do not, indeed, propagate our principles with the sword of power; but there is one sense in which we are propagandists. We cannot help being so. Our example is contagious. In the section of this great country where I live, on the banks of the mighty Mississippi River, we have the true emblem of the tree of liberty. There you may see the giant cotton-wood spreading his branches widely to the winds of heaven. Sometimes the current lays bare his roots, and you behold them extending far around, and penetrating to an immense depth in the soil. When the season of maturity comes, the air is filled with a cotton-like substance, which floats in every direction, bearing on its light wings the living seeds of the mighty tree. Thus the seeds of freedom have emanated from the tree of our liberties; they fill the air; they are wafted to every part of the habitable globe; and even in the barren sands of tyranny they are destined to take root. The tree of liberty will spring up everywhere, and nations shall recline in its shade.

Senator Foote, of Mississippi, also used this language:—

> Such has been the extraordinary course of events in France and Europe, within the last two months, that the more deliberately we survey the scene which has been spread out before us, and the more rigidly we scrutinise the conduct of its actors, the more confident does our conviction become that the glorious work which has been so well begun cannot possibly fail of complete accomplishment; that the age of tyrants and slavery is rapidly drawing to a close; and that the happy period to be signalised by the universal emancipation of man from the fetters of civil oppression, and the recognition in all countries of the great principles of popular sovereignty, equality, and brotherhood,, at this moment visibly commencing.

Will anyone be surprised, after this, that seventy-seven of the most intelligent young slaves, male and female, in Washington city, honestly taking Mr. Foote and his brother senators at their word, and believing that the age of tyrants and slavery was drawing to a close, banded together, and made an effort to obtain their part in this reign of universal brotherhood?

The schooner *Pearl* was lying in the harbour, and Captain Drayton was found to have the heart of a man. Perhaps he, too, had listened to the addresses on Pennsylvania Avenue, and thought in the innocence of his heart, that a man who really *did* something to promote universal emancipation, was no worse than the men who only made speeches about it.

At any rate, Drayton was persuaded to allow these seventy-seven slaves to secrete themselves in the hold of his vessel, and among them were six children of Paul and Milly Edmondson. The incidents of the rest of the narrative will now be given as obtained from Mary and Emily Edmondson, by the lady in whose family they have been placed by the writer for an education.

Some few preliminaries may be necessary in order to understand the account.

A respectable coloured man, by the name of Daniel Bell, who had purchased his own freedom, resided in the city of Washington. His wife, with her eight children, were set free by her master, when on his death-bed. The heirs endeavoured to break the will, on the ground that he was not of sound mind at the time of its preparation. The magistrate, however, before whom it was executed, by his own personal knowledge of the competence of the man at the time, was enabled to defeat their purpose; the family, therefore, lived as free for some years. On the death of this magistrate, the heirs again brought the case into court, and as it seemed likely to be decided against the family, they resolved to secure their legal rights by flight, and engaged passage on board the vessel of Captain Drayton. Many of their associates and friends, stirred up, perhaps, by the recent demonstrations in favour of liberty, begged leave to accompany them in their flight. The seeds of the cotton-wood were flying everywhere, and springing up in all hearts; so that, on the eventful evening of the 15th of April, 1848, not less than seventy-seven men, women, and children, with beating hearts and anxious secrecy, stowed themselves away in the hold of the little schooner, and Captain Drayton was so wicked that he could not, for the life of him, say "Nay" to one of them.

Richard Edmondson had long sought to buy his liberty; had toiled for it early and late; but the price set upon him was so high that he despaired of ever earning it. On this evening he and his three brothers thought, as the reign of universal brotherhood had begun, and

98

the reign of tyrants and slavery come to an end, that they would take to themselves and their sisters that sacred gift of liberty, which all Washington had been informed, two evenings before, it was the peculiar province of America to give to all nations. Their two sisters, aged sixteen and fourteen, were hired out in families in the city. On this evening Samuel Edmondson called at the house where Emily lived, and told her of the projected plan.

"But what will mother think?" said Emily.

"Don't stop to think of her; she would rather we'd be free than to spend time to talk about her."

"Well, then, if Mary will go, I will."

The girls give as a reason for wishing to escape, that though they had never suffered hardships or been treated unkindly, yet they knew they were liable at any time to be sold into rigorous bondage, and separated far from all they loved.

They then all went on board the *Pearl*, which was lying a little way off from the place where vessels usually anchor. There they found a company of slaves, seventy-seven in number.

At twelve o'clock at night the silent wings of the little schooner were spread, and with her weight of fear and mystery she glided out into the stream. A fresh breeze sprang up, and by eleven o'clock next night they had sailed two hundred miles from Washington, and began to think that liberty was gained. They anchored in a place called Cornfield Harbour, intending to wait for daylight. All laid down to sleep in peaceful security, lulled by the gentle rock of the vessel and the rippling of the waters.

But at two o'clock at night they were roused by terrible noises on deck, scuffling, screaming, swearing, and groaning. A steamer had pursued and overtaken them, and the little schooner was boarded by an infuriated set of armed men. In a moment, the captain, mate, and all the crew, were seized and bound, amid oaths and dreadful threats. As they, swearing and yelling, tore open the hatches on the defenceless prisoners below, Richard Edmondson stepped forward, and in a calm voice said to them, "Gentlemen, do yourselves no harm, for we are all here." With this exception, all was still among the slaves as despair could make it; not a word was spoken in the whole company. The men were all bound and placed on board the steamer; the women were left on board the schooner, to be towed after.

The explanation of their capture was this:—In the morning after they had sailed, many families in Washington found their slaves missing, and the event created as great an excitement as the emancipation of France had, two days before. At that time they had listened in the most complacent manner to the announcement that the reign of slavery was near its close, because they had not the slightest idea that the language meant anything; and they were utterly confounded by this practical application of it. More than a hundred men, mounted upon horses, determined to push out into the country, in pursuit of these new disciples of the doctrine of universal emancipation. Here a coloured man, by the name of Judson Diggs, betrayed the whole plot. He had been provoked, because, after having taken a poor woman, with her luggage, down to the boat, she was unable to pay the twenty-five cents that he demanded. So he told these admirers of universal brotherhood that they need not ride into the country, as their slaves had sailed down the river, and were far enough off by this time. A steamer was immediately manned by two hundred armed men, and away they went in pursuit.

When the cortege arrived with the captured slaves, there was a most furious excitement in the city. The men were driven through the streets bound with ropes, two and two. Showers of taunts and jeers rained upon them from all sides. One man asked one of the girls if she "didn't feel pretty to be caught running away," and another asked her "if she wasn't sorry."

She answered, "No, if it was to do again tomorrow, she would do the same."

The man turned to a bystander and said—"Han't she got good spunk?"

But the most vehement excitement was against Drayton and Sayres, the captain and mate of the vessel. Ruffians armed with dirk-knives and pistols crowded around them, with the most horrid threats. One of them struck so near Drayton as to cut his ear, which Emily noticed as bleeding. Meanwhile there mingled in the crowd multitudes of the relatives of the captives, who, looking on them as so many doomed victims, bewildered and lamented them. A brother-in-law of the Edmondsons was so overcome when he saw them that he fainted away and fell down in the street, and was carried home insensible. The sorrowful news. spread to the cottage of Paul and Milly Edmondson; and knowing that all their children were now probably doomed to the Southern market, they gave themselves up to sorrow. "Oh, what a day that was!" said the old mother, when describing that scene to the writer. "Never a morsel of anything could I put into my mouth. Paul and me, we fasted and prayed before the Lord, night and day, for our poor children!"

The whole public sentiment of the community was roused to the most intense indignation. It was repeated from mouth to mouth that they had been kindly treated and never abused; and what could have induced them to try to get their liberty? All that Mr. Stanton had said of the insensible influence of American institutions, and all his pretty similes about the cottonwood seeds, seemed entirely to have escaped the memory of the community, and they could see nothing but the most unheard-of depravity in the attempt of these people to secure freedom. It was strenuously advised by many that their owners should not forgive them—that no mercy should be shown; but that they should be thrown into the hands of the traders, forthwith, for the Southern market—that Siberia of the irresponsible despots of America.

When all the prisoners were lodged in jail, the owners came to make oath to their property, and the property also was required to make oath to their owners. Among them came the married sisters of Mary and Emily, but were not allowed to enter the prison. The girls looked through the iron grates of the third-storey windows, and saw their sisters standing below in the yard weeping.

The guardian of the Edmondsons, who acted in the place of the real owner, apparently touched with their sorrow, promised their family and friends, who were anxious to purchase them, if possible, that they should have an opportunity the next morning. Perhaps he intended at the time to give them one; but, as Bruin and Hill, the keepers of the large slave warehouse in Alexandria, offered him four thousand five hundred dollars for the six children, they were irrevocably sold before the next morning. Bruin would listen to no terms which any of their friends could propose. The lady with whom Mary had lived offered a thousand dollars for her, but Bruin refused, saying he could get double that sum in the New Orleans market. He said he had had his eye upon the family for twelve years, and had the promise of them should they ever be sold.

While the girls remained in the prison they had no beds nor chairs, and only one blanket each, though the nights were chilly; but understanding that the rooms below, where their brothers were confined, were still colder, and that no blankets were given them, they sent their own down to them. In the morning they were allowed to go down into the yard for a few moments; and then they used to run to the window of their brothers' room, to bid them good morning, and kiss them through the grate.

At ten o'clock, Thursday night, the brothers were handcuffed, and, with their sisters, taken into carriages by their new owners, driven to Alexandria, and put into a prison called a Georgia Pen. The girls were put into a large room alone, in total darkness, without bed or blanket, where they spent the night in sobs and tears, in utter ignorance of their brothers' fate. At eight o'clock in the morning they were called to breakfast, when, to their great comfort, they found their four brothers all in the same prison.

They remained here about four weeks, being usually permitted by day to stay below with their brothers, and at night to return to their own rooms. Their brothers had great anxieties about them, fearing they would be sold South. Samuel, in particular, felt very sadly, as he had been the principal actor in getting them away. He often said he would gladly *die* for them, if that would save them from the fate he feared. He used to weep a great deal, though he endeavoured to restrain his tears in their presence.

While in the slave-prison they were required to wash for thirteen men, though their brothers performed a great share of the labour. Before they left, their size and height were measured by their owners. At length they were again taken out, the brothers handcuffed, and all put on board a steamboat, where were about forty slaves, mostly men, and taken to Baltimore. The voyage occupied one day and a night. When arrived in Baltimore, they were thrown into a slave-pen kept by a partner of Bruin and Hill. He was a man of coarse habits, constantly using the most profane language, and grossly obscene and insulting in his remarks to women. Here they were forbidden to pray together, as they had previously been accustomed to do.

But, by rising very early in the morning, they secured to themselves a little interval which they could employ, uninterrupted, in this manner. They, with four or five other women in the prison, used to meet together before daybreak to spread their sorrows before the Refuge of the afflicted; and in these prayers the hard-hearted slave-dealer was daily remembered. The brothers of Mary and Emily were very gentle and tender in their treatment of their sisters, which had an influence upon other men in their company.

At this place they became acquainted with Aunt Rachel, a most godly woman, about middle age, who had been sold into the prison away from her husband. The poor husband used often to come to the prison and beg the trader to sell her to *his* owners, who he thought were willing to purchase her, if the price was not too high. But he was driven off with brutal threats and curses. They remained in Baltimore about three weeks.

The friends in Washington, though hitherto unsuccessful in their efforts to redeem the family, were still exerting themselves in their behalf; and one evening a message was received from them by telegraph, stating that a person would arrive in the morning train of cars prepared to bargain for the family, and that a part of the money was now ready. But the trader was inexorable; and in the morning, an hour before the cars were to arrive, they were all put on board the brig *Union*, ready to sail for New Orleans. The messenger came, and brought nine hundred dollars in money, the gift of a grandson of John Jacob Astor. This was finally appropriated to the ransom of Richard Edmondson, as his wife and children were said to be suffering in Washington; and the trader would not sell the girls to them upon any consideration, nor would he even suffer Richard to be brought back from the brig, which had not yet sailed. The bargain was, however made, and the money deposited in Baltimore.

On this brig the eleven women were put in one small apartment, and the thirty or forty men in an adjoining one. Emily was very seasick most of the time, and her brothers feared she would die. They used to come and carry her out on deck and back again, buy little comforts for their sisters, and take all possible care of them.

Frequently head-winds blew them back, so that they made very slow progress; and in their prayer-meetings, which they held every night, they used to pray that head-winds might blow them to New York; and one of the sailors declared that if they could get within one hundred miles of New York, and the slaves would stand by him, he would make way with the captain, and pilot them into New York himself.

When they arrived near Key West, they hoisted a signal for a pilot, the captain being aware of the dangers of the place, and yet not knowing how to avoid them. As the pilot-boat approached, the slaves were all fastened below, and a heavy canvas thrown over the grated hatchway door, which entirely excluded all circulation of air, and almost produced suffocation. The captain and pilot had a long talk about the price, and some altercation ensued, the captain not being willing to give the price demanded by the pilot; during which time there was great suffering below. The women became so exhausted that they were mostly helpless; and the situation of the men was not much better, though they managed with a stick to break some holes through the canvass on their side, so as to let in a little air, but a few only of the strongest could get there to enjoy it.

Some of them shouted for help as long as their strength would permit; and at length, after what seemed to them an almost interminable interview, the pilot left, refusing to assist them; the canvas was removed, and the brig obliged to turn tack, and take another course. Then one after another, as they got air and strength, crawled out on deck. Mary and Emily were carried out by their brothers as soon as they were able to do it.

Soon after this the stock of provisions ran low, and the water failed, so that the slaves were restricted to a gill a day. The sailors were allowed a quart each, and often gave a pint of it to one of the Edmondsons for their sisters; and they divided it with the other women, as they always did every nice thing they got in such ways.

The day they arrived at the mouth of the Mississippi a terrible storm arose, and the waves rolled mountain high, so that, when the pilot-boat approached, it would sometimes seem to be entirely swallowed by the waves, and again it would emerge, and again appear wholly buried. At length they were towed into and up the river by a steamer, and there, for the first time, saw cotton plantations, and gangs of slaves at work on them.

They arrived at New Orleans in the night, and about ten the next day were landed and marched to what they called the show-rooms, and, going out into the yard, saw a great many men and women sitting around, with such sad faces that Emily soon began to cry, upon which an overseer stepped up and struck her on the chin, and bade her "stop crying, or he would give her something to cry about." Then pointing, he told her "there was the calaboose, where they whipped those who did not behave themselves." As soon as he turned away, a slave-woman came and told her to look cheerful, if she possibly could, as it would be far better for her. One of her brothers soon came to inquire what the woman had been saying to her; and when informed, encouraged Emily to follow the advice, and endeavoured to profit by it himself.

That night all the four brothers had their hair cut close, their moustaches shaved off, and their usual clothing exchanged for a blue jacket and pants, all of which so altered their appearance that at first their sisters did not know them. Then, for three successive days, they were all obliged to stand in an open porch fronting the street, for passersby to look at, except, when one was tired out, she might go in for a little time, and another take her place. Whenever buyers called, they were paraded in the auction-room in rows, exposed to coarse jokes and taunts. When anyone took a liking to any girl in the company, he would call her to him, take hold of her, open her mouth, look at her teeth, and handle her person rudely, frequently making obscene remarks; and she must stand and bear it, without resistance. Mary and Emily complained to their brothers that they could not submit to such treatment. They conversed about it with Wilson, a partner of Bruin and Hill, who had the charge of the slaves at this prison. After this they were treated with more decency.

Another brother of the girls, named Hamilton, had been a slave in or near New Orleans for sixteen years, and had just purchased his own freedom for one thousand dollars; having once before earned that sum for himself, and then had it taken from him. Richard being now really free, as the money was deposited in Baltimore for his ransom, found him out the next day after their arrival at New Orleans, and brought him to the prison to see his brothers and sisters. The meeting was overpoweringly affecting.

He had never before seen his sister Emily, as he had been sold away from his parents before her birth.

The girls' lodging-room was occupied at night by about twenty or thirty women, who all slept on the bare floor, with only a blanket each. After a few days, word was received (which was *really incorrect*), that half the money had been raised for the redemption of Mary and Emily. After this they were allowed, upon their brothers' earnest request, to go to their free brother's house and spend their nights, and return in the mornings, as they had suffered greatly from the mosquitoes and other insects, and their feet were swollen and sore.

While at this prison some horrible cases of cruelty came to their knowledge, and some of them under their own observation. Two persons, one woman and one boy, were whipped to death in the prison while they were there, though they were not in the same pen, or owned by the same trader, as themselves.

None of the slaves were allowed to sleep in the daytime, and sometimes little children sitting or standing idle all day would become so sleepy as not to be able to hold up their eyelids; but, if they were caught thus by the overseer, they were cruelly beaten. Mary and Emily used to watch the little ones, and let them sleep until they heard the overseers coming, and then spring and rouse them in a moment.

One young woman, who had been sold by the traders for the worst of purposes, was returned, not being fortunate (?) enough to suit her purchaser; and, as is their custom in such cases, was most cruelly flogged—so much so that some of her flesh mortified, and her life was despaired of. When Mary and Emily first arrived at New Orleans they saw and conversed with her. She was then just beginning to sit up; was quite small, and very fine-looking, with beautiful straight hair, which was formerly long, but had been cut off short by her brutal tormentors.

The overseer who flogged her said, in their hearing, that he would never flog another girl in that way—it was too much for anyone to bear. They suggest that perhaps the reason why he promised this was because he was obliged to be her nurse, and of course saw her sufferings. She was from Alexandria, but they have forgotten her name.

One young man and woman of their company in the prison, who were engaged to be married, and were sold to different owners, felt so distressed at their separation that they could not or did not labour well; and the young man was soon sent back, with the complaint that he would not answer the purpose. Of course, the money was to be refunded, and he flogged. He was condemned to be flogged each night for a week; and, after about two hundred lashes by the overseer, each one of the male slaves in the prison was required to come and lay on five lashes with all his strength, upon penalty of being flogged himself. The young woman, too, was soon sent there, with a note from her new mistress, requesting that she might be whipped a certain number of lashes, and enclosing the money to pay for it; which request was readily complied with.

While in New Orleans they saw gangs of women cleaning the streets, chained together, some with a heavy iron ball attached to the chain; a form of punishment frequently resorted to for household servants who had displeased their mistresses.

Hamilton Edmondson, the brother who had purchased his own freedom, made great efforts to get good homes for his brothers and sisters in New Orleans, so that they need not be far separated from each other. One day Mr. Wilson, the overseer, took Samuel away with him in a carriage, and returned without him. The brothers and sisters soon found that he was sold, and gone they knew not whither; but they were not allowed to weep, or even look sad, upon pain of severe punishment. The next day, however, to their great joy, he came to the prison himself, and told them he had a good home in the city with an

106

Englishman, who had paid a thousand dollars for him.

After remaining about three weeks in this prison, the Edmondsons were told that in consequence of the prevalence of the yellow fever in the city, together with their not being acclimated, it was deemed dangerous for them to remain there longer; and, besides this, purchasers were loath to give good prices under these circumstances. Some of the slaves in the pen were already sick; some of them old, poor, or dirty, and for these reasons greatly exposed to sickness. Richard Edmondson had already been ransomed, and must be sent back; and, upon the whole, it was thought best to fit out and send off a gang to Baltimore without delay.

The Edmondsons received these tidings with joyful hearts, for they had not yet been undeceived with regard to the raising of the money for their ransom. Their brother who was free procured for them many comforts for the voyage, such as a mattress, blankets, sheets, and different kinds of food and drink; and, accompanied to the vessel by their friends there, they embarked on the brig *Union* just at night, and were towed out of the river. The brig had nearly a full cargo of cotton, molasses, sugar, &c., and, of course, the space for the slaves was exceedingly limited. The place allotted the females was a little, close, filthy room, perhaps eight or ten feet square, filled with cotton within two or three feet of the top of the room, except the space directly under the hatchway door.

Richard Edmondson kept his sisters upon deck with him, though without a shelter; prepared their food himself, made up their bed at night on the top of barrels, or wherever he could find a place, and then slept by their side. Sometimes a storm would arise in the middle of the night, when he would spring up and wake them, and, gathering up their bed and bedding, conduct them to a little kind of a pantry, where they could all three just stand, till the storm passed away. Sometimes he contrived to make a temporary shelter for them out of bits of boards, or something else on deck.

After a voyage of sixteen days, they arrived at Baltimore, fully expecting that their days of slavery were numbered. Here they were conducted back to the same old prison from which they had been taken a few weeks before, though they supposed it would be but for an hour or two. Presently Mr. Bigelow, of Washington, came for Richard. When the girls found that they were not to be set free too, their grief and disappointment were unspeakable. But they were *separated*—Richard to go to his home, his wife and children, and they to remain in the slave-prison. Wearisome days and nights again rolled on. In the mornings they were obliged to march round the yard to the music of fiddles, banjos, &c.; in the daytime they washed and ironed for the male slaves, slept some, and wept a great deal. After a few weeks their father came to visit them, accompanied by their sister.

His object was partly to ascertain what were the very lowest terms upon which their keeper would sell the girls, as he indulged a faint hope that in some way or other the money might be raised, if time enough were allowed. The trader declared he should soon send them to some other slave-market, but he would wait two weeks, and, if the friends could raise the money in that time, they might have them.

The night their father and sister spent in the prison with them, he lay in the room over their heads; and they could hear him groan all night, while their sister was weeping by their side. None of them closed their eyes in sleep.

In the morning came again the wearisome routine of the slave-prison. Old Paul walked quietly into the yard, and sat down to see the poor slaves marched around. He had never seen his daughters in such circumstances before, and his feelings quite overcame him. The yard was narrow, and the girls, as they walked by him, almost brushing him with their clothes, could just hear him groaning within himself, "O my children! my children!"

After the breakfast, which none of them were able to eat, they parted with sad hearts, the father begging the keeper to send them to New Orleans, if the money could not be raised, as perhaps their brothers there might secure for them kind masters.

Two or three weeks afterwards Bruin and Hill visited the prison, dissolved partnership with the trader, settled accounts, and took the Edmondsons again in their own possession.

The girls were roused about eleven o'clock at night, after they had fallen asleep, and told to get up directly, and prepare for going home. They had learned that the word of a slaveholder is not to be trusted, and feared they were going to be sent to Richmond, Virginia, as there had been talk of it. They were soon on their way in the cars with Bruin, and arrived at Washington at a little past midnight.

Their hearts throbbed high when, after these long months of weary captivity, they found themselves once more in the city where were their brothers, sisters, and parents. But they were permitted to see none of them, and were put into a carriage and driven immediately to the slave-prison at Alexandria, where, about two o'clock at night, they found themselves in the same forlorn old room in which they had begun their term of captivity!

This was the latter part of August. Again they were employed in washing, ironing, and sewing by day, and always locked up by night. Sometimes they were allowed to sew in Bruin's house, and even to eat there. After they had been in Alexandria two or three weeks, their eldest married sister, not having heard from them for some time, came to see Bruin, to learn, if possible, something of their fate; and her surprise and joy were great to see them once more, even there. After a few weeks their old father came again to see them. Hopeless as the idea of their emancipation seemed, he still clung to it. He had had some encouragement of assistance in Washington, and he purposed to go North to see if anything could be done there; and he was anxious to obtain from Bruin what were the very lowest possible terms for which he would sell the girls. Bruin drew up his terms in the following document, which we subjoin:—

Alexandria, Va., Sept. 5, 1848.

The bearer, Paul Edmondson, is the father of two girls, Mary Jane and Emily Catherine Edmondson. These girls have been purchased by us, and once sent to the South; and, upon the positive assurance that the money for them would be raised if they were brought back, they were returned. Nothing, it appears, has as yet been done in this respect by those who promised, and we are on the very eve of sending them South the second time; and we are candid in saying that, if they go again, we will not regard any promises made in relation to them. The father wishes to raise money to pay for them; and intends to appeal to the liberality of the humane and the good to aid him, and has requested us to state in writing the conditions upon which we will sell his daughters.

We expect to start our servants to the South in a few days; if the sum of twelve hundred (1200) dollars be raised and paid to us in fifteen days, or we be assured of that sum, then we will retain them for twenty-five days more, to give an opportunity for the raising of the other thousand and fifty (1050) dollars; otherwise we shall be compelled to send them along with our other servants.

Bruin & Hill.

Paul took his papers, and parted from his daughters sorrowfully. After this, the time to the girls dragged on in heavy suspense. Constantly they looked for letter or message, and prayed to God to raise them up a deliverer from some quarter. But day after day and week after week passed, and the dreaded time drew near. The preliminaries for fitting up the gang for South Carolina commenced. Gay calico was bought for them to make up into "show dresses," in which they were to be exhibited on sale. They made them up with far sadder feelings than they would have sewed on their own shrouds. Hope had almost died out of their bosoms. A few days before the gang were to be sent off, their sister made them a sad farewell visit. They mingled their prayers and tears, and the girls made up little tokens of remembrance to send by her as parting gifts to their brothers and sisters, and aged father and mother; and with a farewell sadder than that of a death-bed, the sisters parted.

The evening before the coffle was to start drew on. Mary and Emily went to the house to bid Bruin's family goodbye. Bruin had a little daughter who had been a pet and favourite with the girls. She clung round them, cried, and begged them not to go. Emily told her that if she wished to have them stay, she must go and ask her father. Away ran the little pleader, full of her errand; and was so very earnest in her importunities, that he, to pacify her, said he would consent to their remaining, if his partner, Captain Hill, would do so. At this time Bruin, hearing Mary crying aloud in the prison, went up to see her. With all the earnestness of despair, she made her last appeal to his feelings. She begged him to make the case his own, to think of his own dear little daughter—what if she were exposed to be torn away from every friend on earth, and cut off from all hope of redemption, at the very moment, too, when deliverance was expected! Bruin was not absolutely a man of stone, and this agonising appeal brought tears to his eyes.

He gave some encouragement that, if Hill would consent, they need not be sent off with the gang. A sleepless night followed, spent in weeping, groaning, and prayer. Morning at last dawned; and, according to orders received the day before, they prepared themselves to go, and even put on their bonnets and shawls, and stood ready for the word to be given. When the very last tear of hope was shed, and they were going out to join the gang, Bruin's heart relented. He called them to him, and told them they might remain! Oh, how glad were their hearts made by this, as they might *now* hope on a little longer! Either the entreaties of little Martha or Mary's plea with Bruin had prevailed.

Soon the gang was started on foot—men, women, and children, two and two, the men all handcuffed together, the right wrist of one to the left wrist of the other, and a chain passing through the middle from the handcuffs of one couple to those of the next. The women and children walked in the same manner throughout, handcuffed or chained. Drivers went before and at the side, to take up those who were sick or lame. They were obliged to set off *singing!* accompanied with fiddles and banjos!—"*For they that carried us away captive required of us a song, and they that wasted us required of us mirth.*" And this is a scene of daily occurrence in a Christian country! and Christian ministers say that the right to do these things is *given by God himself!!*

Meanwhile poor old Paul Edmondson went northward to supplicate aid. Anyone who should have travelled in the cars at that time might have seen a venerable-looking black man, all whose air and attitude indicated a patient humility, and who seemed to carry a weight of overwhelming sorrow, like one who had long been acquainted with grief. That man was Paul Edmondson.

Alone, friendless, unknown, and, worst of all, black, he came into the great bustling city of New York, to see if there was anyone there who could give him twenty-five hundred dollars to buy his daughters with. Can anybody realise what a poor man's feelings are, who visits a great, bustling, rich city, alone and unknown, for such an object? The writer has now, in a letter from a slave father and husband who was visiting Portland on a similar errand, a touching expression of it:

> I walked all day, till I was tired and discouraged. O! Mrs. S—, when I see so many people who seem to have so many more things than they want or know what to do with, and then think that I have worked hard, till I am past forty, all my life, and don't own even my own wife and children, it makes me feel sick and discouraged!

So sick at heart and discouraged felt Paul Edmondson. He went to the Anti-Slavery Office, and made his case known. The sum was such a large one, and seemed to many so exorbitant, that though they pitied the poor father, they were disheartened about raising it. They wrote to Washington to authenticate the particulars of the story, and wrote to Bruin and Hill to see if there could be any reduction of price. Meanwhile the poor old man looked sadly from one adviser to another. He was recommended to go to the Rev. H. W. Beecher, and tell his story.

He inquired his way to his door—ascended the steps to ring the door-bell, but his heart failed him: he sat down on the steps, weeping!

There Mr. Beecher found him. He took him in, and inquired his story. There was to be a public meeting that night to raise money. The hapless father begged him to go and plead for his children. He did go, and spoke as if he were pleading for his own father and sisters. Other clergymen followed in the same strain, the meeting became enthusiastic, and the money was raised on the spot, and poor old Paul laid his head that night on a grateful pillow—not to sleep, but to give thanks!

Meanwhile the girls had been dragging on anxious days in the slave-prison. They were employed in sewing for Bruin's family, staying sometimes in the prison, and sometimes in the house.

It is to be stated here that Mr. Bruin is a man of very different character from many in his trade. He is such a man as never would have been found in the profession of a slave-trader, had not the most respectable and religious part of the community defended the right to buy and sell, as being conferred by God himself. It is a fact, with regard to this man, that he was one of the earliest subscribers to the *National Era,* in the District of Columbia; and when a certain individual there brought himself into great peril by assisting fugitive slaves, and there was no one found to go bail for him, Mr. Bruin came forward and performed this kindness.

While we abhor the horrible system and the horrible trade with our whole soul, there is no harm, we suppose, in wishing that such a man had a better occupation. Yet we cannot forbear reminding all such that, when we come to give our account at the judgment-seat of Christ, every man must speak *for himself alone;* and that Christ will not accept as an apology for sin the word of all the ministers and all the synods in the country. He has given fair warning, "*Beware of false prophets;*" and if people will not beware of them, their blood is upon their own heads.

The girls, while under Mr. Bruin's care, were treated with as much kindness and consideration as could possibly consist with the design of selling them. There is no doubt that Bruin was personally friendly to them, and really wished most earnestly that they might be ransomed; but then he did not see how he was to lose two thousand five hundred dollars. He had just the same difficulty on this subject that some New York members of churches have had, when they have had slaves brought into their hands as security for Southern debts. He was sorry for them, and wished them well, and hoped Providence would provide for them when they were sold, but still he could not afford to lose his money; and while such men remain elders and communicants in churches in NewYork, we must not be surprised that there remain slave-traders in Alexandria.

It is one great art of the enemy of souls to lead men to compound for their participation in one branch of sin by their righteous horror of another. The slave-trader has been the general scapegoat on whom all parties have vented their indignation, while buying of him and selling to him.

There is an awful warning given in the fiftieth Psalm to those who in word have professed religion and indeed consented to iniquity, where from the judgment-seat Christ is represented as thus addressing them:—

What hast *thou* to do to declare my statutes, or that thou shouldst take my covenant into thy mouth, seeing thou hatest instruction, and castest my words behind thee? When thou sawest a thief, then thou consentedst with him, and hast been partaker with adulterers.

One thing is certain, that all who do these things, openly or secretly, must, at last, make up their account with a Judge who is no respecter of persons, and who will just as soon condemn an elder in the church for slave-trading as a professed trader; nay, He may make it more tolerable for the Sodom and Gomorrah of the trade than for them—for it may be, if the trader had the means of grace that they have had, that he would have repented long ago.

But to return to our history.—The girls were sitting sewing near the open window of their cage, when Emily said to Mary, "There, Mary, is that white man we have seen from the North." They both looked, and in a moment more saw their own dear father. They sprang and ran through the house and the office, and into the street, shouting as they ran, followed by Bruin, who said he thought the girls were crazy. In a moment they were in their father's arms, but observed that he trembled exceedingly, and that his voice was unsteady. They eagerly inquired if the money was raised for their ransom.

Afraid of exciting their hopes too soon, before their free papers were signed, he said he would talk with them soon, and went into the office with Mr. Bruin and Mr. Chaplin. Mr. Bruin professed himself sincerely glad, as undoubtedly he was, that they had brought the money; but seemed much hurt by the manner in which he had been spoken of by the Rev. H. W. Beecher at the liberation meeting in New York, thinking it hard that no difference should be made between him and other traders, when he had shown himself so much more considerate and humane than the great body of them. He, however, counted over the money and signed the papers with great good will, taking out a five-dollar gold piece for each of the girls, as a parting present.

The affair took longer than they supposed, and the time seemed an age to the poor girls, who were anxiously walking up and down outside the room, in ignorance of their fate. Could their father have brought the money? Why did he tremble so? Could he have failed of the money, at last? Or could it be that their dear mother was dead, for they had heard that she was very ill!

At length a messenger came shouting to them, "You are free, you are free!" Emily thinks she sprang nearly to the ceiling overhead. They jumped, clapped their hands, laughed and shouted aloud. Soon their father came to them, embraced them tenderly, and attempted to quiet them, and told them to prepare themselves to go and see their mother. This they did they know not how, but with considerable help from the family, who all seemed to rejoice in their joy. Their father procured a carriage to take them to the wharf, and, with joy overflowing all bounds, they bade a most affectionate farewell to each member of the family, not even omitting Bruin himself. The "good that there is in human nature" for once had the upper hand, and all were moved to tears of sympathetic joy. Their father, with subdued tenderness, made great efforts to soothe their tumultuous feelings, and at length partially succeeded.

When they arrived at Washington, a carriage was ready to take them to their sister's house. People of every rank and description came running together to get a sight of them. Their brothers caught them up in their arms, and ran about with them, almost frantic with joy. Their aged and venerated mother, raised up from a sick-bed by the stimulus of the glad news, was there, weeping and giving thanks to God. Refreshments were prepared in their sister's house for all who called, and amid greetings and rejoicings, tears and gladness, prayers and thanksgivings, but without sleep, the night passed away, and the morning of November 4, 1848, dawned upon them free and happy.

This last spring, during the month of May, as the writer has already intimated, the aged mother of the Edmondson family came on to New York, and the reason of her coming may be thus briefly explained. She had still one other daughter, the guide and support of her feeble age, or, as she calls her, in her own expressive language, "the last drop of blood in her heart." She had also a son, twenty-one years of age, still a slave on a neighbouring plantation. The infirm woman in whose name the estate was held was supposed to be drawing near to death, and the poor parents were distressed with the fear that, in case of this event, their two remaining children would be sold for the purpose of dividing the estate, and thus thrown into the dreaded Southern market. No one can realise what a constant horror the slave-prisons and the slave-traders are to all the unfortunate families in the vicinity. Everything for which other parents look on their children with pleasure and pride is to these poor souls a source of anxiety and dismay, because it renders the child so much more a merchantable article.

It is no wonder, therefore, that the light in Paul and Milly's cottage was overshadowed by this terrible idea.

The guardians of these children had given their father a written promise to sell them to him for a certain sum, and by hard begging he had acquired a hundred dollars towards the twelve hundred which were necessary. But he was now confined to his bed with sickness. After pouring out earnest prayer to the Helper of the helpless, Milly says, one day she said to Paul, "I tell ye, Paul, I'm going up to New York myself, to see if I can't get that money."

"Paul says to me, 'Why, Milly dear, how can you? Ye an't fit to be off the bed, and ye's never in the cars in your life.'

"Never you fear, Paul,' says I; 'I shall go trusting in the Lord; and the Lord, He'll take me, and He'll bring me, that I know.'

"So I went to the cars and got a white man to put me aboard; and, sure enough, there I found two Bethel ministers; and one set one side o' me, and one set the other, all the way; and they got me my tickets, and looked after my things, and did everything for me. There didn't anything happen to me all the way. Sometimes, when I went to set down in the sitting-rooms, people looked at me and moved off so scornful! Well, I thought, I wish the Lord would give you a better mind."

Emily and Mary, who had been at school in New York State, came to the city to meet their mother, and they brought her directly to the Rev. Henry W. Beecher's house, where the writer then was.

The writer remembers now the scene when she first met this mother and daughters. It must be recollected that they had not seen

115

each other before for four years. One was sitting each side the mother, holding her hand; and the air of pride and filial affection with which they presented her was touching to behold. After being presented to the writer, she again sat down between them, took a hand of each, and looked very earnestly first on one and then on the other; and then looking up, said, with a smile, "Oh, these children! how they do lie round our hearts!"

She then explained to the writer all her sorrows and anxieties for the younger children. "Now, madam," she says, "that man that keeps the great trading-house at Alexandria, *that man,*" she said with a strong, indignant expression, "has sent to know if there's any more of my children to be sold. That man said he wanted to see *me!* Yes, ma'am, he said he'd give twenty dollars to see me. I wouldn't see him if he'd give me a hundred! He sent for me to come and see him when he had my daughters in his prison. I wouldn't go to see him; I didn't want to see them there!"

The two daughters, Emily and Mary, here became very much excited, and broke out in some very natural but bitter language against all slaveholders. "Hush, children! you must forgive your enemies," she said.

"But they're so wicked!" said the girls.

"Ah, children, you must hate—the *sin,* but love the *sinner.*"

"Well," said one of the girls, "mother, if I was taken again and made a slave of, I'd kill myself."

"I trust not, child; that would be wicked."

"But, mother, I *should;* I know I never could bear it."

"Bear it, my child!" she answered, "it's they that bears the sorrow here is they that has the glories there."

There was a deep, indescribable pathos of voice and manner as she said these words; a solemnity and force, and yet a sweetness, that can never be forgotten.

This poor slave-mother, whose whole life had been one long outrage on her holiest feelings; who had been kept from the power to read God's Word, whose whole pilgrimage had been made one day of sorrow by the injustice of a Christian nation, she had yet learned to solve the highest problem of Christian ethics, and to do what so few reformers can do—hate the *sin,* but love the *sinner!*

A great deal of interest was excited among the ladies in Brooklyn by this history. Several large meetings were held in different parlours, in which the old mother related her history with great simplicity and pathos, and a subscription for the redemption of the remaining two of her family, was soon on foot. It may be interesting to know that the subscription-list was headed by the lovely and benevolent Jenny Lind Goldschmidt.

Some of the ladies who listened to this touching story were so much interested in Mrs. Edmondson personally, they wished to have her daguerreotype taken, both that they might be strengthened and refreshed by the sight of her placid countenance, and that they might see the beauty of true goodness beaming there.

She accordingly went to the rooms with them, with all the simplicity of a little child. "Oh," said she to one of the ladies, "you can't think how happy it's made me to get here, where everybody is *so kind* to me! Why, last night, when I went home, I was so happy I couldn't sleep. I had to go and tell my Saviour, over and over again, how happy I was."

A lady spoke to her about reading something. "Law bless you, honey! I can't read a letter."

"Then," said another lady, "how have you learned so much of God and heavenly things?"

"Well, 'pears like a *gift* from above."

"Can you have the Bible read to you?"

"Why, yes; Paul, he reads a little, but then he has so much work all day, and when he gets home at night he's so tired! and his eyes is bad. But the *Sperit* teaches us."

"Do you go much to meeting?"

"Not much now, we live so far. In winter I can't never. But, oh! what meetings I have had, alone in the corner—my Saviour and only me!" The smile with which these words were spoken was a thing to be remembered. A little girl, daughter of one of the ladies, made some rather severe remarks about somebody in the daguerreotype rooms, and her mother checked her.

The old lady looked up, with her placid smile. "That puts me in mind," she said, "of what I heard a preacher say once. 'My friends,' says he, 'if you know of anything that will make a brother's heart glad, *run quick and tell it;* but if it is something that will only cause a sigh, bottle it up, bottle it up!' Oh, I often tell my children, 'Bottle it up, bottle it up!' "

When the writer came to part with the old lady, she said to her, "Well, goodbye, my dear friend; remember and pray for me."

"Pray for *you!*" she said, earnestly. "Indeed I shall; I can't help it."

She then, raising her finger, said, in an emphatic tone, peculiar to the old of her race, "Tell you what: we never gets no good bread ourselves till we begins *to ask for our brethren.*"

The writer takes this opportunity to inform all those friends, in different parts of the country, who generously contributed for the redemption of these children, that they are *at last free!*

The following extract from the letter of a lady in Washington may be interesting to them:—

I have seen the Edmondson parents—Paul and his wife Milly. I have seen the free Edmondsons—mother, son, and daughter—the very day after the great era of free life commenced, while yet the inspiration was on them, while the mother's face was all light and love, the father's eyes moistened and glistening with tears, the son calm in conscious manhood and responsibility, the daughter (not more than fifteen years old, I think) smiling a delightful appreciation of joy in the present and hope in the future, thus suddenly and completely unfolded.

Thus have we finished the account of one of the families who were taken on board the *Pearl.* We have another history to give, to which we cannot promise so fortunate a termination.

The Fugitives of the Pearl

Contents

The Fugitives of the Pearl

(Extract from The Journal of Negro History Volume 1)

The traditional history of the Negro in America, during nearly three hundred years, is one in which the elements of pathos, humour and tragedy are thoroughly mixed and in which the experiences encountered are of a kind to grip the hearts and consciences of men of every race and every creed. Just as colonial Americans resented their enforced enlistment for maritime service under the flag of King George, so it may be assumed that with equal vigour did the little band of Africans object to a forced expatriation from their native wilds, even though, as it happened, they were destined to be, in part, the builders of a great and prosperous nation and the progenitors of a strong and forward-looking race.

There are few incidents that distinguish the bondage of the descendants of that first boat load of involuntary African explorers, that evince, in so large a degree the elements alluded to, as do those which cluster about the story of the "Edmondson Children." There were altogether fourteen sons and daughters of Paul and Amelia who passed as devoutly pious and respectable old folks. Paul was a freeman who hired his time in the city. Amelia was a slave. Their little cabin, a few miles out of the city of Washington proper, was so neat and orderly that it was regarded as a model for masters and slaves alike for many miles around. They were thus permitted to live together by the owners of Amelia, who realized how much more valuable the children would be as a marketable group after some years of such care and attention as the mother would be sure to bestow.

Milly, as she was familiarly called, reared the children, tilled the garden, and, being especially handy with the needle, turned off many a job of sewing for the family of her mistress. She was entirely ignorant so far as books go, but Paul read the Bible to her when visiting his loved ones on Sunday and what he explained she remembered and treasured up for comfort in her moments of despair.

The older boys and girls were hired out in prominent families in the city and by their intelligence, orderly conduct and other evidences of good breeding came to be known far and wide as "The Edmondson Children," the phrase being taken as descriptive of all that was excellent and desirable in a slave. The one incurable grief of these humble parents was that in bringing children into the world they were helping to perpetuate the institution of slavery. The fear that any day might bring to them the cruel pangs of separation and the terrible knowledge that their loved ones had been condemned to the horrors of the auction block was with them always a constant shadow, darkening each waking moment.

More and ever more, they were torn with anxiety for the future of the children and so they threw themselves with increasing faith and dependence upon the Master of all, and no visit of the children was so hurried or full of other matters but that a few moments were reserved for prayer.

At their departure, one after another was clasped to the mother's breast and always this earnest admonition followed them, "Be good children and the blessed Lord will take care of you." Louisa and Joseph, the two youngest, were still at home when there occurred events in which several of their older brothers and sisters took so prominent a part and which are here to be related.

The incidents of this narrative which are reflected in its title are contemporary with and in a measure resultant from the revolution out of which came the establishment of the first French Republic and the expulsion of Louis-Philippe in 1848. The citizens of the United States were felicitating their brothers across the water upon the achievement of so desirable a result. In Washington especially, the event was joyously acclaimed. Public meetings were held at which representatives of the people in both houses of Congress spoke encouragingly of the recent advance toward universal liberty. The city was regally adorned with flags and bunting and illumination and music everywhere.

The White House was elaborately decorated in honour of the event and its general observance, scheduled for April 13. A procession of national dignitaries, local organizations and the civic authorities, accompanied by several bands of music and throngs of citizens, made its way to the open square (now Lafayette Park) opposite the White House. Speeches were in order. Among the addresses which aroused the large crowd to enthusiasm were those of Senator Patterson of Tennessee and Senator Foote of Mississippi. [1] The former likened the Tree of Liberty to the great cotton-wood tree of his section, whose seed is blown far and wide, while the latter spoke eloquently of the universal emancipation of man and the approaching recognition in all countries of the great principles of equality and brotherhood.

Here and there huddled unobtrusively in groups on the fringe of the crowd were numbers of slaves. The enthusiasm of the throng, frequently manifested in shouts of approval, was discreetly reflected in the suppressed excitement of the slaves, who whispered among themselves concerning the curious and incredible expressions they had heard. Could it possibly be that these splendid truths, this forecast of universal liberty, might include them too? A few of the more intelligent, among whom was Samuel Edmondson, drew together to discuss the event and were not long concluding that the authority they had listened to could not be questioned and that they should at once contribute their share towards so desirable a consummation.

Coincident with, this celebration there had arrived at Washington the schooner *Pearl* with Daniel Drayton[2] as super-cargo, Captain Sayres, owner, and a young man, Chester English, as sailor and cook. Drayton witnessed the great demonstration near the White House and, as might have been expected, the sentiment that seemed to have won all Washington found a natural and active response, for when the news of the purpose of his visit was communicated by the woman for whose deliverance he had agreed to make the trip, he was appealed to on behalf of others and consented to take all who should be aboard

---

1. The Washington Union, April 14, 1848.
2 Daniel Drayton was a native of New Jersey who had spent several years following the water. He had risen from cook to captain in the wood-carrying business from the Maurice River to Philadelphia. Eventually he engaged in coast traffic from Philadelphia southward. He seemed to have drifted quite naturally from strong humane impulses, intensified by an old-time spiritual conversion, into a settled conviction that the fatherhood of God and the brotherhood of man was a reality and that it was his duty to do what he could to assist those in bondage. Latterly his voyages had carried him into the Chesapeake Bay and thence up the Potomac. His first successful effort to assist the slaves was made on an earlier trip when he agreed to take away a woman and five children. The husband was already a free man. The woman had under an agreement with her master more than paid for her liberty, but when she had asked for a settlement, he had only answered by threatening to sell her. The mother and five children were taken aboard at night and after ten days were safely delivered at Frenchtown, where the husband was in waiting for them. Memoir of Daniel Drayton, Congressional Library.

by ten o'clock that night.

The Edmondson boys actively promoted the scheme and, rightly in so just a cause, abused the privileges which their integrity and unusual intelligence had won for them. The news was passed to an aggregate of 77 persons, all of whom faithfully appeared and were safely stowed away between decks before midnight. Samuel sought his sisters Emily and Mary at their places of employment and acquainted them with his purpose. They at first hesitated on account of the necessity of leaving without seeing their mother, but were soon persuaded that it was an opportunity they should not be willing to neglect.

The *Pearl* cast free from her moorings shortly after midnight Saturday and silently, with no sign of life aboard, save running lights fore and aft, crept out to mid-stream and made a course towards the lower Potomac. The condition that obtained on Sunday morning after the discovery of the absence of so many slaves from their usual duties may be accurately described as approaching a panic. Had the evidences of a dreadful plague become as suddenly manifest, the community could not have experienced a greater sense of horror or for the moment been more thoroughly paralyzed. A hundred or more families were affected through the action of these seventy and seven slaves and the stern proofs of their flight were many times multiplied.

The action of the masters in this emergency is eloquent testimony that the fine orations of two days before concerning the spread of liberty and universal brotherhood had been nothing more than so many meaningless conversations. When confronted on Sunday morning with the fact that theirs and their neighbours' slaves, in so great numbers, had disappeared during the night, the realization of the difference between popular enthusiasm for a sentiment and a real sacrifice for a principle, was borne in upon them and they found that while they enjoyed the former they were not at all ready to espouse the latter.

As a result the day was but little advanced when an excited cavalcade of the masters, after scouring every portion of the city, broke for the open country to the North, designing to cover each of the roads leading from the city. They had not reached the District limits, however, when they whirled about and galloped furiously in the opposite direction and never checked rein, until panting and foaming, their horses were brought up at the wharves. A vessel was chartered and steamed away almost immediately on its mission to capture the party of runaway slaves.

Fate, which occasionally plays such strange and cruel tricks in the lives of men, presented in this instance a Machiavellian combination of opposing forces, that was disastrous to the enterprise of the fugitives. Judson Diggs,[3] one of their own people, a man who in all reason might have been expected to sympathize with their effort, took upon himself the role of Judas. Judson was a drayman and had hauled some packages to the wharf for one of the slaves, who was without funds to pay the charge, and although he was solemnly promised that the money should be sent him, he proceeded at once to wreak vengeance through a betrayal of the entire party.

Even so, it would seem they might have had an excellent chance to escape, but for the adverse winds and tides which set against them towards the close of Sunday. They were approaching the open waters of the Bay and the little vessel was already pitching and tossing as from the lashing of a gale. The captain decided that it was the part of prudence to remain within the more quiet waters of the Potomac for the night and make the open sea by light of day. Under these circumstances they put into Cornfield Harbor and here in the quiet hours before midnight the pursuing masters found them.

It is difficult to realize the consternation felt by the fugitives when the noise of tramping feet and the voices of angry men broke upon their ears. They seemed to realize at once that they were lost and many gave themselves up to shrieks and tears until wise council prevailed. Captain Drayton and his mate were immediately the storm centre of the infuriated masters, many of whom were loud in the demand that summary vengeance be wreaked upon them and that these two at least should be hung from the yard arm. It was easily possible that this demand might have been acceded to, had not a diversion been caused by some of the others who were anxious to locate the slaves.

To satisfy themselves as to their safety they proceeded to break open the hatchways when, so suddenly as to create something of a panic, Richard Edmondson bounded on deck and in a voice of sup-

---

3. The only punishment meted out to Judson Diggs for his act of betrayal, so far as is known, was that by a party of young men who, shortly after the occurrence, took him from his cart and after considerable rough handling, threw him into the little stream that in those days and indeed for many years thereafter, took its way along the north side of the old John Wesley Church, then located at a spot directly opposite the north corner of the Convent of the Sacred Heart on Connecticut Avenue, between L and M Streets. A number of old citizens now living distinctly remember Judson Diggs, who lived, despised and avoided, until late in the sixties. One of these is Mr. Jerome A. Johnson of the Treasury Department.

pressed excitement exclaimed, "Do yourselves no harm, gentlemen, for we are all here!" Richard was young, muscular and of splendid proportions and seeing him thus by the poor light of smoky lanterns, with flashing eyes and swinging arms, leaping into their midst with an unknown number of others following, some of the masters experienced a feeling of terror, and dropping their guns, scurried away to safety among the dark shadows of the vessel.

By the time the others reached the deck, the shock of Richard's strange appearance had somewhat died away and when Samuel, who was one of the last, appeared, a sharp blow which, but for a sudden lurch of the vessel, would have laid him low fell on one side of his head. Drayton and Sayres, [4] who were witnesses of this incident, were horrified to think that, having not so much as a penknife with which to defend themselves, these poor creatures might be brutally murdered, and, notwithstanding the serious aspect of their own fortunes, [5] protested vigorously against such violence. But for this timely interference, there is but little doubt that some of these poor people would have been cruelly if not fatally injured.

The true condition of affairs, however, was speedily recognised and seeing there was nothing to fear in the way of resistance, order was soon evolved out of the general chaos and then came the decision to make an early start on the return trip. Among the slaves, the reaction from a feeling of hope and joyous anticipation of the delights of freedom was terrible indeed. The bitter gall and wormwood of failure was the sad and gloomy portion of these seventy and seven souls. Among them then there were but few who were not completely crushed, their minds a seething torrent, in which regret, misery and despair made battle for the mastery. Children weeping and wailing clung to the skirts of their elders. The women with shrieks, groans and tearful lamentations deplored their sad fate, while the men, securely chained wrist and wrist together, stood with heads dropped forward, too dazed

---

4. *Memoir of Daniel Drayton*, Congressional Library.
5. The case against Drayton and Sayres was prosecuted by Philip Barton Key, the District Attorney, before Judge Crawford, and on appeal the prisoners were sentenced to pay a fine of $10,000 and to remain in jail until the same should be paid. English was absolved from all criminal responsibility and given his liberty. After an imprisonment of more than four years they were pardoned by President Filmore, to whom such application had been presented by Charles Sumner. *Memoir of Daniel Drayton*. The fare at the jail was insufficient and of poor quality and a more wholesome and generous diet was frequently surreptitiously furnished by Susannah Ford, a coloured woman, who sold lunches in the lobby of the Court House.

and wretched for aught but to turn their stony gaze within upon the wild anguish of their aching hearts.

Their arrival at Washington was signalized by a demonstration vastly different but little short of that which had taken place a few days before. The wharves were alive with an eager and excited throng all intent upon a view of the miserable folks who had been guilty of so ungrateful an effort. So disorderly was the mob that the debarkation was for some time delayed. This was finally accomplished through the strenuous efforts of the entire constabulary of the city.

The utmost watchfulness and care was, however, unavailing to prevent assaults. The most serious instance of this kind was the act of an Irish ruffian, who so far forgot the traditions and sufferings of his own people as to cast himself upon Drayton with a huge dirk and cut off a piece of his ear. [6] For a few moments all the horrors incident to riot and bloodshed were in evidence. The air was filled with the screams of terrorized women and children and the curses and threats of vengeful men. The whole was a struggling, swaying mass, which for a season had been swept beyond itself by brutish passion.

Numerous arrests were made and in due course the march to the jail was begun with the accompanying crowd hurling taunts and jeers at every step. While they were proceeding thus, an onlooker said to Emily, "Aren't you ashamed to run away and make all this trouble for everybody?"

To this she replied, "No sir, we are not and if we had to go through it again, we'd do the same thing."

The controversy that was precipitated through the attempted escape, between the advance guard of abolition and the defenders of slavery, was most bitter and violent. The storm broke furiously about the offices of The National Era. In Congress, Mr. Giddings of Ohio moved an "inquiry into the cause of the detention at the District jail of persons merely for attempting to vindicate their inalienable rights. "Senator Hale of New Hampshire moved a resolution of "inquiry into the necessity for additional laws for the protection of property in the District." [7]

A committee consisting of such notable characters as the Channings, Samuel May, Samuel Howe, Eichard Hildreth, Samuel Sewell and Eobert Morris Jr., was formed at Boston to furnish aid and defense for Drayton. These men were empowered to employ counsel

---

6. Stowe, *Key to Uncle Tom's Cabin.*
7. *The National Era,* April 16, 1848.

and collect money. Horace Mann, Wm. H. Seward, Salmon P. Chase and Fessenden of Maine volunteered to serve gratuitously. [8]

Other philanthropists directed their attention to the liberation of these slaves. The Edmondsons were owned by an estate. The administrator, who was approached by John Brent, [9] the husband of the oldest sister of the children, agreed to give their friends an opportunity to effect their purchase, as he was unwilling to run any further risk by keeping them. He failed to keep this promise and when Mr. Brent went to see them the next day he was informed that they had been sold to Bruin and Hill, the slave-dealers of Alexandria and Baltimore and had been sent to the former city. A cash sum of $4,500 had been accepted for the six children and when taxed with the failure to keep his promise, he simply said he was unwilling to take any further risk with them. Bruin also refused to listen to any proposals, saying he had long had his eyes on the family and could get twice what he paid for them in the New Orleans market.

They were first taken to the slave pens at Alexandria, where they remained nearly a month. Here the girls were required to do the washing for a dozen or more men with the assistance of their brothers and were at length put aboard a steamboat and taken to Baltimore where they remained three weeks. Through the exertions of friends at Washington, $900 was given towards their freedom by a grandson of John Jacob Astor, and this was appropriated towards the ransom of Richard, as his wife and children were said to be ill and suffering at Washington. The money arrived on the morning they were to sail for New Orleans but they had all been put aboard the brig *Union*, which was ready to sail, and the trader refused to allow Richard to be taken off.

The voyage to New Orleans covered a period of seven days, during which much discomfort and suffering were experienced. There were eleven women in the party, all of whom were forced to live in

---

8. *Memoir of Daniel Drayton.*

9. John Brent, the husband of Elizabeth, the oldest of the Edmondson girls, had first bought himself, earning the money chiefly by sawing wood; had then bought the freedom of his father, Elton Brent, for whom he paid $800, and finally bought Elizabeth's freedom, after which they were married. He purchased the ground at the southwest corner of 18th and L streets, now owned by his heirs, and erected a small frame dwelling. This was later enlarged and there the John Wesley A. M. E. Zion Church was established. He was a labourer in the War Department during forty years and died in 1885. From interviews with Mr. Brent and other members of the family.

one small apartment and the men numbering thirty-five or forty, in another not much larger. Most of them being unaccustomed to travel by water were afflicted with all the horrors of seasickness.

Emily's suffering from this cause was most pitiable and so serious was her condition at one time that the boys feared she would die. The brothers, however, as in all circumstances, were very kind and would tenderly carry her out on deck whenever the heat in their close quarters became too oppressive and would buy little comforts that were in their reach and minister in all possible ways to her relief.

In due course they arrived at New Orleans and were immediately initiated into the horrors of a Georgia pen. The girls were required to spend much time in the show room, where purchasers came to examine them carefully with a view to buying them. On one occasion a youthful dandy had applied for a young person whom he wished to install as housekeeper and the trader decided that Emily would just about meet the requirements, but when he called her she was found to be indulging in a fit of weeping. The youth, therefore, refused to consider her, saying that he had no room for the snuffles in his house. The loss of this transaction so incensed the trader, who said he had been offered $1,500 for the proper person, that he slapped Emily's face and threatened to send her to the calaboose, if he found her crying again.

Here also the boys had their hair closely cropped and their clothes, which were of good material, exchanged for suits of blue-jeans. Appearing thus, they were daily exhibited on the porch for sale. Richard, who was in reality free, as his purchase money was on deposit in Baltimore, was allowed to come and go at will and early bent his energies toward the discovery of their elder brother Hamilton, [10] who was living somewhere in the city. His quest was soon rewarded with success and one day to the delight of his sisters and brothers he brought him to see them.

Hamilton had never seen Emily, as he had been sold away from his parents before her birth, but his joy, though mingled with sorrow, could not be suppressed. He was soon busy with plans for the increase of their meagre comforts. Finding upon inquiry that Hamilton was thoroughly responsible, the trader consented to the girls spending

---

10. Hamilton Edmondson was sold in the New Orleans slave market about the year 1840 and took the name of his purchaser and was thereafter known as Hamilton Taylor. He learned the trade of cooper and was allowed a percentage of his earnings, but was unfortunate in having his first savings stolen. He eventually acquired his freedom through the payment of $1,000.

their nights at their brother's home. He was also at pains to secure good homes for the unfortunate group and was successful in inducing a wealthy Englishman to purchase his brother Samuel.

In consequence of an epidemic of yellow fever, which increased in virulence from day to day, the traders decided to bring the slaves North without further delay and so a few days later they were re-embarked on the brig Union with Baltimore as their destination. Samuel was the only one of the brothers and sisters left behind. As he was pleasantly situated with humane and kindly owners, the parting from him was not so sad as otherwise it might have been. Sixteen days were required for the trip and upon their arrival they were again placed in the same old prison. Richard was almost immediately freed and, in company with a Mr. Bigelow, of Washington, was enabled to rejoin his wife and children.

Paul Edmondson visited his children at the Baltimore jail in company with their sister.[11] He had been encouraged to hope that in some way a fund might be raised for their ransom, but it was not until some weeks later, after they had been returned through Washington and again placed in their old slave quarters at Alexandria, that an understanding as to terms could be had with Bruin and Hill. They finally agreed to accept $2,250 if the amount was raised within a certain time and gave Paul a signed statement of the terms, which might be used as his credentials in the matter of soliciting assistance. Armed with this document, he arrived at New York and found his way to the Anti-Slavery office, where the price demanded was considered so exorbitant that but little encouragement was given him. From here he went to the home of Rev. Henry Ward Beecher, where he arrived foot-sore and weary. After ringing the bell, he sat upon the doorstep weeping. Here Mr. Beecher found him and, taking him into his library, inquired his story.

As a result there followed a public meeting in Mr. Beecher's Brooklyn church, at which he pleaded passionately as if for his own children, while other clergymen spoke with equal interest and feeling. The money was raised, an agent appointed to consummate the ransom of the children, and Paul, with a sense of happiness and relief

---

11. He continued in the cooperage business, was highly respected and became comparatively wealthy, having a place of business on Girard near Camp street. John S. Brent, who is his nephew and the son of the John Brent heretofore mentioned in this narrative, spent a week with his uncle, Hamilton Taylor, in 1865, on his return from Texas, when, as a member of the Fifth Massachusetts Cavalry, he was mustered out of the service. Interview with John S. Brent.

to which he had long been a stranger, started with the good news on his way homeward.

Meanwhile the girls were torn with doubt and anxiety as to the success of their father's mission. Several weeks had elapsed and the traders were again getting together a come of slaves for shipment to the slave market, this time to that in South Carolina. The girls too, had been ordered to be in readiness and the evening before had broken down in tears when Bruin's young daughter, who was a favourite with the girls, sought them out and pleaded with them not to go. Emily told her to persuade her father not to send them and so she did, while clinging around his neck until he had not the heart to refuse.

A day or two later, while looking from their window, they caught sight of their father and ran into his arms shouting and crying. So great was their joy that they did not notice their father's companion, a Mr. Chaplin, the agent appointed at the New York meeting to take charge of the details of their ransom. These were soon completed, their free papers signed and the money paid over. Bruin, too, it is said, was pleased with the joy and happiness in evidence on every hand and upon bidding the girls goodbye gave each a five dollar gold piece.

Upon their arrival at Washington they were taken in a carriage to their sister's home, whence the news of their deliverance seemed to have penetrated to every corner of the neighbourhood with the result that it was far into the night before the last greetings and congratulations had been received and they were permitted, in the seclusion of the family circle, to kneel with their parents in prayer and thanksgiving. [12]

In the meantime what had become of Samuel? When Hamilton

12 The fame of the Edmondson children through the incident of the *Pearl* was now wide indeed, and after the Brooklyn meeting there had been made many suggestions looking to their education and further benefit. The movement for the education of Emily and Mary was crystallized into a definite proposition and they were both placed in a private school a short distance out of New York. Miss Myrtilla Miner had already established her school for girls at Washington and had moved to a new location at about what is now the square bounded by 19th, 20th, N and O streets. Here, after returning from New York, Emily assisted Miss Miner in the school and it was in one of the little cabins on this place that the Edmondson family established their home after moving in from the country. Miss Miner, speaking of the establishment of her school at its new location, says: "Emily and I lived here alone, unprotected except by God, the rowdies occasionally stoning the house at evening and we nightly retired in the expectation that the house would be fired before morning. Emily and I have been seen practicing shooting with a pistol." Myrtilla Miner, *A Memoir*, Congressional Library; *Key to Uncle Tom's Cabin*.

Edmondson was seeking to locate his sisters and brothers in desirable homes in New Orleans, he first saw Mr. Horace Cammack, a prosperous cotton merchant, whose friendship and respect he had long since won and who, upon the further representation of Samuel's proficiency as a butler, agreed to purchase him. In this wise, it came to pass that Samuel was duly installed as upper houseman in the Cammack home. Although situated more happily than most slaves he was fully determined, as ever, that the world should one day know and respect him as a free man, and patiently waited and watched for the opportunity to accomplish his purpose.

Meanwhile another element had thrust itself into the equation and must be reckoned with in the solution of the problem of his afterlife. It happened that Mrs. Cammack, a lady of much beauty and refinement of manner, had in her employ as maid, a young girl of not more than eighteen years named Delia Taylor. She was tall, graceful and winsome, of the clear *mulatto* type, and through long service in close contact with her mistress, had acquired that refinement and culture, which elicit the admiration and delight of those in like station and inspire a feeling much akin to reverence in those more lowly placed. With some difficulty Samuel approached her with a proposal and, although at first refused, finally won her as his bride.

Matters now moved along on pleasant lines for Samuel

The parents of the children, however, were not yet entirely relieved of the fears that had so long haunted them, for there were still the two youngest children, Louisa and Joseph, whom the good mother frequently alluded to as "the last two drops of blood in her heart," and although she had scarcely ever seen a railroad train, she determined to go to New York herself to see what could be done and to thank the good people who had already brought so much of happiness to herself and family. While the mother was in that city the girls were brought to see her and in later years she often delighted to tell of their happy meeting and of the good white folks who were brought together to hear her story. She returned to Washington at the end of a week, carrying the assurance that the money would be provided for the redemption of the last two of her children.

Mrs. Louisa Joy, the last of the "Edmondson Children," died only a short while ago, (as at time of first publication, and Delia during several months, but with the advent of Master Tom, Cammack's son who had been away to college, there was encountered an element of discord, which was for a while to destroy their happiness. This young gentleman took a violent dislike to Samuel from the very first meal the latter served him. They finally clashed and Samuel had to run away. His master, however, sent his would-be-oppressor with the rest of the family to the country and ordered Samuel to return home. This he did and immediately entered upon his duties.

The year following, Mr. Cammack went to Europe on cotton business and not long after his arrival was killed in a violent storm while yachting with friends off the coast of Norway. After this event, affairs in the life of Samuel gradually approached a crisis, while in the meantime an additional responsibility had been added to himself and Delia in the person of a little boy, whom they named David.

Master Tom, being now the head of the house, left little room for doubt as to the authority he had inherited and proceeded to evince the same in no uncertain way, especially towards those against whom he held a grievance. To get rid of Samuel was first in order. This was the easiest possible matter, for there was not a wealthy family on the visiting list of the Cammacks who would not, even at some sacrifice, make a place for him in their service. Through the close intimacy of Mrs. Cammack and Mrs. Slidell, the latter was given the refusal and Samuel told to go around and see his future mistress. To her he expressed a desire to serve in her employ but he was now determined more than ever that his next master should be himself. Accordingly he proceeded directly to a friend from whom he purchased a set of free-papers, which had been made out and sold him by a white man. These required that he should start immediately up the river but upon a full consideration of the matter he decided that the risks were too great in that direction. The problem was a serious one. An error of judgment, a step in the wrong direction, would not only be a serious, if not fatal blow to his hopes, but might lead to untold hardships to others most dear to him.

Somewhat irresolutely he turned his steps towards the river front, gazing with longing eyes at the stretch of water, the many ships in harbour, some entering, others steaming away or being towed out to open water. The thought that in this direction, beyond the wide seas, lay his refuge and ultimate hope came to him with so much force as to cause him to reel like one on whom a severe blow had been dealt. He stood for some time, seemingly bewildered, in the din and noise of the wharf, noting abstractedly the many bales of cotton, as truck after truck-load was rushed aboard an outward bound steamer. The bales seemed to fascinate him completely.

A stevedore yelled at him to move out of the way and aroused him into action, but in that interval an idea which seemed to offer a possible means of escape had been evolved. He would impersonate a merchant from the West Indies in search of a missing bale of goods and endeavour to get passage to the Islands, where he well knew the flag of free England was abundant guarantee for his protection. The main thought seemed a happy one, for he soon found a merchantman that was to clear that night for Jamaica. It was not a passenger vessel, but the captain, a good-natured Briton, said that he had an extra bunk in the cabin and if the gentleman did not mind roughing it, he would be glad to have his company. The first step towards his freedom was successfully taken, the money paid down for the passage and with the injunction from the captain to be aboard by nine o'clock he returned ashore.

Only a few hours now remained to him, before a long, perhaps a lasting separation from his dear wife and baby, and thinking to pass these with them he hurried thence by the most unfrequented route, but had hardly crossed the threshold when Delia, weeping bitterly, implored him to make good his escape, as Master Tom had already sent the officers to look for him. With a last fond embrace and a tear, which, falling upon that cradled babe, meant present sorrow, but no less future hope, the husband and father made his way under the friendly shadows of the night, back to the waiting ship.

When the officer from the custom house came aboard to inspect the ship's papers Samuel was resting, apparently without concern, in the upper bunk of the little cabin.

The captain seated himself at the centre table, opposite the officer, and spread the papers before him. "Heigho, I see you have a passenger this trip," and then read from the sheet: "Samuel Edmondson, Jamaica, W. I., thirty years old. General Merchant."

"Yes," said the captain as he concluded. "Mr. Edmondson asked for passage at the last moment and as he was alone and we had a bunk not in service, I thought I'd take him along. He has a valuable bale of goods astray, probably at Jamaica, and is anxious to return and look it up."

"Well I hope he may find it. Where is he? let's have a look at him."

"Mr. Edmondson, will you come this way a moment?" called the captain.

As may be imagined the subject of this conversation had been listening intently and now when it was demanded that he present himself, he murmured a fervent "God help me" and jumped nimbly to the deck.

"This is my passenger," said the captain, and to Samuel he said: "The customs officer simply wished to see you, Mr. Edmondson."

Samuel bowed and stood at ease, resting one hand upon the table and in this attitude without the quiver of an eyelash or the flinching of a muscle, bore the searching look of the officer, which rested first upon his face and then upon his hand. The flush of excitement still mounting his cheek and brow, gave a bronzed swarthiness and decidedly un-American cast to his rich brown colour, while his features, clean-cut and but slightly of the Negro type, with hands well shaped and nails quite clean, were a combination of conditions rarely met in the average slave. The first glance of suspicion was almost immediately lost to view in the smile of friendly greeting with which the officer's hand was extended. "I hope you may recover your goods," were the words he said and, rising, added: "I must be off." The captain had meanwhile placed his liquor chest on the table and, in a glass of good old Jamaica rum, a hearty "*Bon voyage*" and responsive "Good wishes" were exchanged.

The subsequent story of Samuel, interesting and adventurous as it is, scarcely comes within the scope of the purpose of this article. After a brief stay at Jamaica, Samuel sailed before the mast on an English schooner carrying a cargo of dye-wood to Liverpool. Two years were passed here in the service of a wealthy merchant, whom he had served while a guest of his former master in New Orleans. During the third year he was joined by his wife and boy who had been liberated by their mistress. Subsequently the family took passage for Australia under the protection of a relative of his Liverpool employer, who was returning to extensive mining and sheep-raising interests near the rapidly growing city of Melbourne. [13]

John H. Paynter

---

13. Note. This personal narrative of Samuel Edmondson was related by himself at his home in Anacostia where he died several years ago.

LEONAUR

ALSO FROM LEONAUR
AVAILABLE IN SOFTCOVER OR HARDCOVER WITH DUST JACKET

ESCAPE FROM THE FRENCH *by Edward Boys*—A Young Royal Navy Midshipman's Adventures During the Napoleonic War.

THE VOYAGE OF H.M.S. PANDORA *by Edward Edwards R. N. & George Hamilton, edited by Basil Thomson*—In Pursuit of the Mutineers of the Bounty in the South Seas—1790-1791.

MEDUSA *by J. B. Henry Savigny and Alexander Correard and Charlotte-Adélaïde Dard* —Narrative of a Voyage to Senegal in 1816 & The Sufferings of the Picard Family After the Shipwreck of the Medusa.

THE SEA WAR OF 1812 VOLUME 1 *by A. T. Mahan*—A History of the Maritime Conflict.

THE SEA WAR OF 1812 VOLUME 2 *by A. T. Mahan*—A History of the Maritime Conflict.

WETHERELL OF H. M. S. HUSSAR *by John Wetherell*—The Recollections of an Ordinary Seaman of the Royal Navy During the Napoleonic Wars.

THE NAVAL BRIGADE IN NATAL *by C. R. N. Burne*—With the Guns of H. M. S. Terrible & H. M. S. Tartar during the Boer War 1899-1900.

THE VOYAGE OF H. M. S. BOUNTY *by William Bligh*—The True Story of an 18th Century Voyage of Exploration and Mutiny.

SHIPWRECK! *by William Gilly*—The Royal Navy's Disasters at Sea 1793-1849.

KING'S CUTTERS AND SMUGGLERS: 1700-1855 *by E. Keble Chatterton*—A unique period of maritime history-from the beginning of the eighteenth to the middle of the nineteenth century when British seamen risked all to smuggle valuable goods from wool to tea and spirits from and to the Continent.

CONFEDERATE BLOCKADE RUNNER *by John Wilkinson*—The Personal Recollections of an Officer of the Confederate Navy.

NAVAL BATTLES OF THE NAPOLEONIC WARS *by W. H. Fitchett*—Cape St. Vincent, the Nile, Cadiz, Copenhagen, Trafalgar & Others.

PRISONERS OF THE RED DESERT *by R. S. Gwatkin-Williams*—The Adventures of the Crew of the Tara During the First World War.

U-BOAT WAR 1914-1918 *by James B. Connolly/Karl von Schenk*—Two Contrasting Accounts from Both Sides of the Conflict at Sea D uring the Great War.

CPSIA information can be obtained
at www.ICGtesting.com
Printed in the USA
BVHW04164825O423
663034BV00009B/35/J

9 781782 821342